Economic Development Issues:
Greece, Israel, Taiwan, Thailand

September 1968

Supplementary Paper No. 25 issued by the
COMMITTEE FOR ECONOMIC DEVELOPMENT

A CED SUPPLEMENTARY PAPER

This Supplementary Paper is issued by the Research and Policy Committee of the Committee for Economic Development in conformity with the CED Bylaws (Art. V, Sec. 6), which authorize the publication of a manuscript as a Supplementary Paper if:

a) It is recommended for publication by the Project Director of a subcommittee because in his opinion, it "constitutes an important contribution to the understanding of a problem on which research has been initiated by the Research and Policy Committee" and,

b) It is approved for publication by a majority of an Editorial Board on the ground that it presents "an analysis which is a significant contribution to the understanding of the problem in question."

This Supplementary Paper relates to the Statement on National Policy, *How Low Income Countries Can Advance Their Own Growth,* issued by the CED Research and Policy Committee in September 1966.

The members of the Editorial Board authorizing publication of this Supplementary Paper were:

RAFAEL CARRION, JR.	*Members of the Research and Policy Committee*
ROBERT C. COSGROVE	*of the Committee for Economic Development*
LLOYD REYNOLDS	*Members of the Research Advisory Board of*
DONALD C. STONE	*the Committee for Economic Development*
ALFRED C. NEAL	*President of the Committee for Economic Development*
ROY BLOUGH	*Project Director of the CED Subcommittee on Development Policy*

This paper has also been read by the Research Advisory Board, the members of which under the CED Bylaws may submit memoranda of comment, reservation, or dissent.

While publication of this Supplementary Paper is authorized by CED's Bylaws, except as noted above its contents have not been approved, disapproved, or acted upon by the Committee for Economic Development, the Board of Trustees, the Research and Policy Committee, the Research Advisory Board, the Research Staff, or any member of any board or committee, or any officer of the Committee for Economic Development.

CED RESEARCH ADVISORY BOARD

Chairman
EDWARD S. MASON
Lamont University Professor
Harvard University

J. DOUGLAS BROWN
Provost and Dean of the Faculty
Emeritus
Industrial Relations Section
Princeton University

OTTO ECKSTEIN
Department of Economics
Harvard University

KERMIT GORDON
President
The Brookings Institution

ARNOLD HARBERGER
Department of Economics
University of Chicago

CHARLES P. KINDLEBERGER
Department of Economics and
 Social Science
Massachusetts Institute of Technology

DANIEL P. MOYNIHAN, Director
Joint Center for Urban Studies of the
 Massachusetts Institute of Technology
 and Harvard University

WALLACE S. SAYRE
Department of Public Law and Government
Columbia University

T. W. SCHULTZ
Department of Economics
University of Chicago

DONALD C. STONE
Dean, Graduate School of Public and
 International Affairs
University of Pittsburgh

MITCHELL SVIRIDOFF, Vice President
Division of National Affairs
The Ford Foundation

RAYMOND VERNON
Professor of International Trade and
 Investment
Graduate School of Business Administration
Harvard University

Economic Development Issues: Greece, Israel, Taiwan, Thailand

Postwar Economic Problems in Greece
Diomedes D. Psilos

The Characteristics of Israel's Economic Growth
Nadav Halevi

The Reasons for Taiwan's High Growth Rate
Shigeto Kawano

Key Factors in the Development of Thailand
Katsumi Mitani

September 1968

Supplementary Paper No. 25 issued by the
COMMITTEE FOR ECONOMIC DEVELOPMENT

Copyright © 1968 by the Committee for Economic Development

All rights reserved. No part of this book may be reproduced or utilized in any form or by any means, electronic or mechanical, including photocopying, recording, or by any information storage and retrieval system, without permission in writing from the Committee for Economic Development, 477 Madison Ave., New York, N.Y. 10022.

Printed in the U.S.A.

First Printing, September 1968
COMMITTEE FOR ECONOMIC DEVELOPMENT
477 Madison Avenue, New York, N.Y. 10022

Library of Congress Catalog Card Number: 68-29783

Foreword

Together with its companion volume entitled *Economic Development Issues: Latin America*, the present publication is the outgrowth of a study conducted by the Committee for Economic Development's Subcommittee on Development Policy regarding the key factors influencing the rate of growth in low-income countries. The subcommittee's findings were presented in the policy statement entitled *How Low Income Countries Can Advance Their Own Growth: The Lessons of Experience*, issued in September 1966 by CED's Research and Policy Committee.

Whereas previous CED policy statements relating to development had dealt largely with the roles of foreign aid, trade, and investment, the subcommittee concentrated its attention on the conditions that must be present within the low-income countries themselves if they are to achieve high rates of growth in per capita income. In attempting to find answers to the question why some low-income countries have been successful in achieving a healthy economic growth while others have not, CED drew heavily on the knowledge and advice of economists from Latin America, Southeast Asia, and the Mediterranean region. These economists were commissioned to prepare studies analyzing for fifteen selected countries the successes and failures of their efforts to achieve economic development.

Having found these papers to be of substantial value in its work, the subcommittee decided to make available to a wider audience those that seemed of general significance. In accordance with procedures established by CED bylaws, the papers were submitted to an editorial board comprised of Trustees and academic advisors to the CED, whose names appear on page III. This volume contains four studies of countries in the Mediterranean and Southeast Asian regions that were approved for publication by a majority of the editorial board.

The four authors represented in this volume have had distinguished careers in the academic world or with economic research centers, and all are intimately familiar with the countries about which they write. Nadav Halevi is Senior Lecturer at the Hebrew University of Jerusalem and has written extensively on Israel's economic development and foreign trade. Shigeto Kawano, Professor of Agricultural Economics at the University of Tokyo, has made studies of Taiwan as well as of Southeast Asian countries generally. Katsumi Mitani, Manager of the Research Division of the Japan Economic Research Institute, served as a research economist in Thailand for the Japanese government. Diomedes D. Psilos has been Director of Research for the Center of Planning and Economic Research in Athens and is now Director General of the Athens Stock Exchange. More information about the authors is to be found in the biographical sketch accompanying each study.

In behalf of CED I would like to acknowledge the invaluable assistance of various organizations and individuals in bringing this volume into being. One of CED's counterpart organizations abroad, Keizai Doyukai in Japan, is owed a particular debt of gratitude for its help in obtaining the services of Messrs. Kawano and Mitani. Frank Brandenburg, formerly of the CED staff, conducted the background research of the Subcommittee on Development Policy and supervised the translations. Carl Rieser, CED Editorial Supervisor, and Karl Schriftgiesser, Associate Director of Information, helped prepare the volume for publication. To the authors is owed a special debt of gratitude for their contributions and particularly for their cooperation in revising and updating for publication the material and statistics in these papers.

Roy Blough, *Project Director*
CED Subcommittee on Development Policy

Contents

Foreword	*Roy Blough*	*VII*
Postwar Economic Problems in Greece	*Diomedes D. Psilos*	*1*
The Characteristics of Israel's Economic Growth	*Nadav Halevi*	*79*
The Reasons for Taiwan's High Growth Rate	*Shigeto Kawano*	*121*
Key Factors in the Development of Thailand	*Katsumi Mitani*	*159*

Economic Development Issues: Greece, Israel, Taiwan, Thailand

September 1968

Supplementary Paper No. 25 issued by the
COMMITTEE FOR ECONOMIC DEVELOPMENT

1.

Postwar Economic Problems in Greece

Diomedes D. Psilos

The Author

DIOMEDES D. PSILOS is an American-trained economist who has held important economic posts in Greece. After graduating from the School of Political Science in Athens, Mr. Psilos came to this country to pursue his studies at the University of California, where he received his doctorate in economics in 1962. He also served as a research associate at the Federal Reserve Bank of San Francisco, taught economics at the University of Maryland, and was a research associate for the Committee for Economic Development. Mr. Psilos returned to Athens in 1962 as a senior economist and research project director for the Center of Economic Research (now the Center of Planning and Economic Research), and since 1965 has been Director General of the Athens Stock Exchange. He is a member of the Capital Market Committee set up in 1962 by the Organization for Economic Cooperation and Development (OECD), and he has represented Greece in various international conferences. Mr. Psilos is the author of a number of economic studies on the financial aspects of development, including *The Choice of Financial Assets in Greece*, *The Capital Market in Greece*, and co-author of *Industrial Capital in Greek Development* (with Howard S. Ellis and Richard M. Westebbe).

Contents

Introduction	5
The Growth Record	7
The Role of Capital Formation	15
The Role of Foreign Trade	23
Trends in Exports and Imports	24
Foreign Aid as a Factor in Greece's Economic Growth	33
The Period Prior to the Truman Doctrine	34
Foreign Aid During 1947–1954	35
Foreign Aid Programs, 1954–1963	38
The Contribution of Foreign Aid to Greece's Economic Growth	44
The Role of Government	52
Public Spending	53
Government Policies Affecting Private Demand	56
Monetary Policy	58
Policies Affecting the Allocation of Resources	64
Memoranda of Comment, Reservation, or Dissent	69
Appendix: Notes on the Difficulties of Economic Planning in Greece	70

Tables

1:	Per Capita Domestic Product, 1958	9
2:	Saving Ratios, Money Supply, and Other Liquid Assets, 1953–66	12
3:	Weighted Rates of Return on Financial Assets	14
4:	Investment Ratios and Marginal Fixed Capital Coefficients	16
5:	Distribution of Private Fixed Investment	16
6:	Distribution of Governmental Investment Expenditures, 1949–64	19
7:	Imports, Exports, and Balance of Trade, 1954–66	24
8:	Selected Imports	26
9:	Imports by Major Categories	26
10:	Inflows of Capital to Greece, 1947–54	36
11:	Inflows of Foreign Aid, 1954–63	42
12:	Total Inflows of Capital for the Public Sector in Greece, 1944–66	44
13:	U.S. Commodity Shipments to Greece Under PL 665 and PL 480	48
14:	Credit Outstanding by Sectors	63

Introduction

The aim of this study is to identify the main factors that had an effect—either positive or negative—on the economic growth of Greece during the entire postwar period through 1966, and to analyze the role of government policy in guiding or influencing these factors. In the chapters that follow, a number of factors that seem to be generally responsible for the rate of growth in the past are discussed in some detail. But before examining the details, it might be helpful to summarize the broad trends and to comment on some specific problems that arise from the high rate of growth in the economy and from the general economic policies which helped bring this about.

The real per capita net national income in Greece rose from about $180 in 1955 to about $420 in 1964, and the rate of growth of gross domestic product (GDP), at constant prices, averaged 7.2 per cent over the 1948–64 period and 8.7 per cent in the last two years. Likewise, industrial and agricultural productivity on the average increased at rates comparable to or even higher than the rates observed in developed western countries. From 1948 to 1964, industrial production increased by 9 per cent, and during 1965–66, it increased by 11.7 per cent annually. Agricultural production increased by 6.2 per cent up to 1964 and by 2 per cent during 1965 and 1966. The construction and service sectors also registered impressively high rates of productivity.

The high growth rates in the real sectors were accompanied by extremely high rates of increases in the financial sector as well, especially after 1953. The stock of money has increased at a rate of 18.6 per cent since 1953, as compared to the 11.5 per cent rate of increase in gross national product (GNP) at current prices, over the same period, reflecting a high rate of monetization in the Greek economy. The liquidity of the banking system, on the other hand, has grown tremendously since 1953, increasing in absolute terms by 32.3 billion drachmas, or at an average annual rate of 29.2 per cent. This rise in liquidity, in the form of deposits other than demand deposits, is one of the most interesting monetary developments in Greece since 1953. Nevertheless, disguised in these monetary developments is the *threat of inflation,* which may come about because of sudden economic and psychological shocks to the system and existing inelasticities in the production sector.

In the opinion of the author, here are the main factors that seem to have affected the over-all rate of growth:

First, the capital formation undertaken by the public and private sector. Indeed, the aggregate investment ratio increased from 15.0 per cent of GNP, at constant prices, in 1948-52 to 20.2 per cent in 1961-64, and, at 1958 prices, it rose to 25.0 per cent in 1965. Private fixed investment rose from 7.3 per cent in 1948-52 to 15.5 per cent in 1965. Of course, this increase in domestic capital formation kept the total demand relatively speaking at high levels, which led to high rates of economic growth. Nevertheless, the distribution of capital funds, especially in the private sector, was not the most desirable one, a fact which weakens the basis for a future high rate of development in this field. For instance, no well-formulated policy has been applied to create the necessary infrastructure in the private sector, nor has there been an effort to establish import-substitute industries, which are the prerequisites for future growth.

Second, the role of the volume and composition of foreign trade. However, though this has been an important factor in the rate of growth, there remains unsolved the chronic problem of the balance-of-payments deficit. Likewise, the contribution of foreign aid in the past was very decisive, but the dependence of Greece on foreign sources for finance still presents an important consideration in future planning in view of the higher capital requirements needed to achieve a self-sustained economic growth. In this connection, some institutional reforms should necessarily take place in Greece in order to facilitate private international financial transactions and to internationalize, so to speak, the Greek capital market. The association of Greece with the European Economic Community (EEC) indeed requires drastic reforms in the capital market.

The Growth Record

As in the case of many other less-developed countries, the Greek economy is hampered by population pressures that are aggravated by an inefficient agricultural system. According to the latest census, the population of Greece was 8.4 million in 1961. The total land area is 130,900 square kilometers, of which the greater part by far comprises barren islands and mountainous regions; arable land is only 28.8 per cent of the total. The overall density of population is thus about 65 persons per square kilometer, and in terms of arable land it is more than 220 persons per square kilometer. Farm units are small, highly fragmented, and self-sufficient, and a high proportion of the total work force is involved in agriculture.

Fortunately, Greece is not subject to the explosive growth in population experienced by many less-developed countries. The Greek population is relatively stable. During the decade of the 1950's the annual growth in population averaged slightly less than 1 per cent, and estimates put the current rate of increase at only about one-half of 1 per cent a year. However, it should be noted that in part at least this decrease is attributable to the rapid rise of emigration, which jumped from a level of about 25,000 people a year at the end of the 1950's to 105,600 in 1964. This is a mixed blessing since emigration deprives Greece of many highly skilled and efficient industrial and agricultural workers at the same time that it reduces the population pressure and cuts down the number of unemployed.*

Although there are no reliable figures on the number of unemployed workers, the available information indicates that the problem of unemployment in Greece is a most serious and urgent one. The census estimate for 1961 put unemployment at 6.5 per cent of the total active working population, while unemployment in the nonagricultural sector was estimated at about 11 per cent. Seasonal unemployment in some agricultural regions has been estimated at between 10 and 25 per cent on an annual basis, which indeed are impressively high figures.[1] Beyond this there is a considerable amount of disguised unemployment in the Greek economy.

The available indexes show a rapid growth in per capita income over the past few years. Real per capita gross national income rose from about $400 in 1961 to about $550 in 1966, an annual average growth rate of 6.6 per cent. The figures for real per capita net national income show a slightly lower rate of growth, but still a rapid one, from $310 in 1958 to about $420 in 1964, an annual average growth rate of 5.2 per cent.[2] However, it is important to point out that the significance of these average growth figures is diminished by the considerable existing inequalities in income among regions as well as among groups. It is particularly important to weigh regional differences in assessing the significance of national averages, a point that is dramatically illustrated in the following table showing the variation among regions in terms of per capita domestic product.

The highly skewed regional distribution of domestic product and also national income in Greece, which has not significantly changed since 1958, stems of course, from the existing differences in natural and human resources as well as in climatic conditions

---

*See Memorandum by CHARLES P. KINDLEBERGER, p. 69.
1. See Andreas G. Papanoreou, *A Strategy for Greek Economic Development* (Athens: Center of Economic Research, 1962), pp. 24–26; and Adam Pepelasis and Pan A. Yotopoulos, *Labor Surplus in Greek Agriculture, 1953–1960* (Athens: Center of Economic Research, 1962).
2. Ministry of Coordination, *National Accounts*; and Bank of Greece, *Report for the Year 1966*.

Table 1: Per Capita Domestic Product, 1958
(in constant 1958 U. S. dollars)

Attica	$494.60
NATIONAL AVERAGE	309.70
Macedonia	283.00
Peloponnese	275.56
Thessaly	259.66
Rest of Mainland and Euboia	241.46
Aegean Islands	223.06
Crete	224.06
Thrace	210.63
Ionian Islands	179.70
Epirus	169.96

Sources: Ministry of Coordination, *National Accounts*; and Center of Planning and Economic Research, Athens.

between the various regions. Nevertheless, government policy in the past has favored the concentration of industrial activity in the main urban areas, the most important being the Athens-Piraeus area, which employs 57 per cent of the total number of industrial laborers and accounts for about 59 per cent of total manufacturing output.

Turning now to the make-up of gross domestic product by sectors, we find that manufacturing accounts for a relatively small portion of the total. Here is the distribution of GDP according to the latest figures available (1965):

	Percentage of Total GDP
Agriculture, forestry, hunting, fishing	23.4%
Mining and quarrying	1.2
Manufacturing	18.2
Construction	7.4
Electricity, gas, water	1.8
Transport, storage, communications	7.5
Wholesale and retail trade	12.5
Banking, insurance, real estate	1.8
Ownership of dwellings	9.5
Public administration and defense	6.0
Services	10.7
Total	100.0

Source: Ministry of Coordination. (These figures are based on constant 1958 prices.)

This distribution of GDP among sectors indicates that structural changes of the Greek economic system are necessary and desirable—particularly in regard to the industrialization of the country—if Greece is to survive in the European Common Market (EEC). Greece became an associate member of EEC in 1962. However, such structural transformation requires a well-planned resource allocation, consistent with the economic and social goals of the country.

Notwithstanding its structural and institutional deficiencies, the Greek economy has registered impressively high rates of growth since 1948. Measured in terms of GDP in constant prices the annual rate of growth of the economy was 7.2 per cent from 1948 to 1964, 6.8 per cent from 1953 to 1958, 6.6 per cent from 1958 to 1964, and 8.7 per cent from the period 1965 to 1966. The rate of increase in industrial and agricultural production also has been highly impressive. Industrial production increased at a rate of 11.3 per cent annually up to 1953; 9.1 per cent during 1953–58; and 7.3 per cent in 1958–64, and during the last two years it increased 11.7 per cent annually. The construction and housing sectors also grew at a fast rate over the entire periods, fluctuating between 9 and 13 per cent annually. Wholesale and retail trade, including banking services, registered an annual average rate of growth of about 7–8 per cent.

Agricultural production rose at an annual rate of 11.3 per cent during 1948–53, but declined to 3.4 per cent in 1953–58, rising slightly to 4.2 per cent during 1953–58, only to decline to 2 per cent during the past two years.

Over the period from 1951 to 1961, output per person in the labor force increased 4.8 per cent per annum for the economy as a whole; by sector, the increase was 6.5 per cent in manufacturing, 4.6 per cent in construction, and 4.6 per cent in agriculture.[3]

It is interesting to note that all the indicators of growth described above compare favorably with those for most of the developed European economies. Annual rates of growth in real GNP over the 1954–61 period were: Austria, 5.8 per cent; Italy,

---

3. *Five-Year Plan 1966–1970*, Center of Planning and Economic Research, Athens, 1965, p. 112.

6.3 per cent; Sweden, 3.8 per cent; Great Britain, 2.6 per cent; and West Germany, 7.1 per cent. Industrial production increases, over the same period averaged 6.4 per cent for Austria, 8.6 per cent for Italy, 8.3 per cent for West Germany, 5.4 per cent for France, and 2.7 per cent for Great Britain.[4] Similarly, Greece's increases in productivity in the industrial and services sectors were higher than in some other European countries. An exception is noted only in agricultural productivity, where Greece lags behind Belgium, France, Germany, Denmark, and other developed countries.

However, despite these impressively high rates of growth in output and productivity, no major structural changes appear to have taken place over the entire postwar period in Greece. For instance, over the period 1950-64, value added by the industrial sector as a share of total value added by the economy as a whole increased by only 3.07 percentage points, rising from 16.93 per cent in 1950 to 20.00 per cent in 1964. (This is in 1954 prices.) The elasticity of manufacturing production, with respect to total production at constant prices, has been estimated at 1.17 for the period 1954-64 and 1.31 for the period 1952-62.

In the financial sector the Greek economy seems to have shown spectacular developments: while per capita incomes are modest, the savings income ratio is high. The marginal propensity to save is .21, which ranks high by any standard.[5] Table 2 shows that the ratio of domestic savings to gross domestic product increased from 13.5 per cent in 1953 to 20.1 per cent in 1965, whereas during the 1950-52 period the savings ratio averaged only 6.6 per cent annually. Private saving also showed a rapid increase, rising from 11.7 per cent to 19.8 of GDP over the 1953-65 period, as against 8.6 per cent average saving ratio in 1950-52. The savings trends in Greece after 1953 compare favorably to saving ratios in other countries. Thus, the ratio of do-

---

4. Organization for Economic Cooperation and Development, *General Statistics*, Paris, September 1962.
5. For the development of this argument, see Diomedes D. Psilos, *Capital Market in Greece*, Research Monography No. 9 (Athens: Center of Economic Research, 1964); and Howard S. Ellis, Diomedes D. Psilos, and Richard Westebbe, *Industrial Capital in Greek Development* (Athens: Center of Economic Research, 1964).

Table 2: Saving Ratios, Money Supply, and Other Liquid Assets, 1953-66
(yearly averages in millions of drachmas)

	Saving/GDP ratios[a] Domestic	Private	Stock of Money	Liquid Assets[b]	Annual Change in Consumer Price Index
1953	13.5%	11.7%	4,093	1,570	9.0%
1954	10.6	9.1	5,395	2,317	15.0
1955	15.5	12.7	6,397	3,226	5.7
1956	15.5	13.1	7,956	4,421	3.7
1957	16.8	13.9	8,903	7,319	2.3
1958	14.3	11.6	10,341	10,292	1.4
1959	16.2	14.1	11,263	13,273	2.3
1960	15.2	13.0	13,658	16,965	2.3
1961	18.8	15.6	15,911	19,850	1.8
1962	18.7	15.2	18,188	25,166	-.3
1963	20.5	17.6	20,883	26,949	3.0
1964	20.6	18.0	25,215	30,794	0.8
1965	20.1	19.8	28,580	33,941	4.8

[a]The saving ratios for the period 1955-57 appear high due to revisions in *National Accounts* in 1966.
[b]Time and savings deposits held by the public.
Sources: Ministry of Coordination, *National Accounts*; and Bank of Greece.

mestic saving to GDP in the United States averaged 18.6 per cent over the period 1950-59; Belgium, 17.6 per cent; Italy, 19.5 per cent; Turkey, 12; Portugal, 11; and Spain, 15 per cent.[6]

The great revival of savings since the early 1950's shows itself in a marked increase of liquidity. The stock of money has increased rapidly since 1953. The annual rate of increase has been 18.6 per cent as compared with the 11.5 per cent annual rate of increase in GNP in current prices over the same period. These changes meant a sharp decline in income velocity, from 12.34 per cent in 1953 to 6.81 per cent in 1965.

The primary forces responsible for the rapid increase of nominal stock of money have been the deficit financing of the agricultural sector, the heavy defense expenditures, and the government's effort to fully utilize the development potential of the economy. Despite this rapid growth of the money supply, however, the cost-of-living index rose at an annual rate of only 1.82 per cent over the 1957-60 period and 2.02 per cent from 1961 to

---

6. United Nations Department of Economic and Social Affairs, *World Economic Survey, 1960* (New York: United Nations, 1961), pp. 19 and 61.

1965. The steep rise earlier, from 1953 to 1956, when the cost of living index rose at an annual rate of 8.16 per cent, was due mainly to the impact of the devaluation of the drachma in 1953.

With the possible exception of 1965, the price trends registered in Greece after 1955-56 compare favorably to price trends in other developed or developing economies, indicating that monetary stability has been restored and that the public has gradually recovered from the psychology of inflation. During the restoration of monetary stability many forces worked themselves out in Greece. In the first place, the continous rise in the volume of invisible foreign exchange receipts, in conjunction with devaluation, contributed to a decline in the rate of inflation, especially after 1955.

Secondly, the accumulation of foreign exchange reserves at the Central Bank made possible the financing of increased imports, primarily foodstuffs and other commodities with inelastic demand, while the liberalization of trade created keen competition in the domestic market, where falling prices of some products induced a wave of bankruptcies of small firms. In addition, the rise in foreign exchange reserves with the Bank of Greece allowed the Bank to stabilize the price of gold sovereigns, which induced people to shift out of this asset after 1956-57 and put their wealth (or savings) into other financial assets such as savings and time deposits and fixed interest securities.[7] That people are willing to convert accumulated gold sovereigns into deposits or other financial assets indicates that the Greek public has gradually recovered from the psychology of inflation. The preference for gold holdings has been diminished still as a consequence of the restrictions imposed by the Bank of Greece on the free gold market in December 1965. Finally, the imports of capital goods after 1954-55 led to higher rates of domestic manufacturing production, with depressing effects upon prices.

---

7. In Greece the preference for holding gold sovereigns until recently affected strongly the rate of inflation. This was true up to 1965, and indeed there still seems to be a close relationship between the price of gold coins and the change in the price index of other commodities, a fact that forces the Bank of Greece to intervene daily in the open market to stabilize the price of gold sovereigns. Hence, a minimum level of foreign exchange reserves is permanently required.

Table 2 shows also that wealth in the form of liquid assets other than money-savings and time deposits rose from 1,570 million drachmas in 1953 to 33,941 million in 1965, increasing at the annual rate of 29.2 per cent as compared to 18.6 per cent annual rate of growth in the stock of money. The ratio of liquid assets to the stock of money rose from .384 in 1953 to 1.19 in 1965, which indicates that the liquidity of the Greek economy has been mostly in forms other than money. This form of liquidity is usually very low in developing countries and very high in developed ones. Hence the Greek economy, from the financial point of view, seems to have started its development process with adequate capital funds. The most important factors accounting for the rapid accumulation of funds in deposit form may be the following: (1) The growth in per capita income, from $180 in 1955 to $420 in 1964; (2) the price stability, which contributed to a higher propensity to save out of current income and encouraged the shift out of gold sovereigns into income earning assets; (3) the lack of securities issues, due to the imperfect organization of the capital market; (4) the tax-incentive system intro-

Table 3: Weighted Rates of Return on Financial Assets

Year	Rate of Return on Deposits[a] %	Yields on Bonds %	Yields on Shares[b] %
1954	7.00	6.01	—
1955	7.00	8.25	—
1956	9.57	7.11	—
1957	8.62	8.49	9.26
1958	7.66	7.05	8.65
1959	6.66	6.26	7.83
1960	4.34	6.61	5.03
1961	4.43	6.36	4.48
1962	4.20	6.22	4.30
1963	4.00	6.50	5.17
1964	4.00	6.50	5.65
1965	4.00	6.91	5.51

[a] Deposits include only time and savings deposits with financial institutions.
[b] Weighted averages for 23 private corporations which paid out dividends constantly over the period 1957-62. For the years 1963-65 the rates are arithmetic averages.

duced in 1955-1956, which exempted income earned on deposits from taxation.

There is also a fifth possible factor; namely the comparatively high rates of return earned on deposits with financial institutions. (See Table 3.) As regards this last factor, of course, no definite statement can be made as to its quantitative influence upon the volume of deposits for the entire period under review. Only in the earlier years would income differentials have been notably decisive. For the whole period, the influence of the nominal and expected real interest rates upon the accumulation of real liquid assets in the form of savings and time deposits has been found to be negative (−.1708 and −.1908 respectively). This is precisely the reverse of what might have been expected if rationality is assumed in a theory of choice. Apparently, liquidity and marketability considerations have been more significant than income considerations in determining portfolio shifts. Furthermore, the size of financial surpluses has been too small to justify shifts between financial assets and to make portfolio adjustments worth while.[8]

In conclusion, the Greek economy has experienced an impressively high rate of growth since the early 1950's, although from the point of view of structure much remains to be done. What were the driving forces behind the increases in productivity and the economy generally? Certain factors that have played a key role in this are discussed in the following chapters.

The Role of Capital Formation

One of the most growth-stimulating factors in any economy is a high rate of capital formation with a suitable composition. This chapter examines the effects of the volume and structure of

---

8. The average size of deposits accounts ranged from 15,000 to 30,000 drachmas over the 1960-62 period, and certainly the size was much smaller in the previous period. See Psilos, *op. cit.*, p. 58.

investment, both private and public, on Greece's productive capacity and growth over the 1949-64 period. Tables 4 and 5 present the key statistics.

Table 4 shows that gross aggregate investment, in constant 1954 prices, increased from 15.0 per cent of GNP during the period 1949-52 to 20.0 per cent in 1961-64. (As noted in the table, this excludes transfers of ships.) This ratio apparently reached the level of 25 per cent in 1965, according to the latest estimates, based on 1958 prices. Although these statistics are of a preliminary nature, fixed investment in 1965 increased considerably, due mainly to large sums invested by a few foreign corporations such as ESSO-PAPAS and LARKO. Over the whole period from 1949 to 1965, private investment in fixed assets rose from 7.3 per cent to about 15.5 per cent of GNP.

Table 4: Investment Ratios[a] and Marginal Fixed Capital Coefficients (at constant 1954 prices)

	Gross Fixed Total Investment as a Percentage of GNP	Private Fixed Investment as a Percentage of GNP	Marginal Fixed Capital Coefficient[b]
1949-52	15.0%	7.3%	3.16%
1953-56	13.6	9.2	2.47
1957-60	17.2	11.9	3.46
1961-64	20.0	13.5	3.69

[a]Excludes transfers of ships.
[b]Measured as the ratio of gross fixed total investment to the change in GNP, at constant prices.

Table 5: Distribution of Private Fixed Investment (at constant prices)

	1949-52	1953-56	1957-60	1961-64
Agriculture	7.6%	6.5%	13.6%	10.8%
Manufacturing and Mining	32.7	16.6	16.9	10.9
Housing	33.8	51.0	42.4	45.3
Transportation and Communications	10.1	8.2	13.8	16.3
Energy and water projects	5.6	3.5	1.9	.8
Other	10.2	14.2	11.4	15.9
Total	100.0	100.0	100.0	100.0

The ratio of total investment and private investment in Greece has been lower than that for other European countries. In Germany, for instance, gross domestic investment over the 1953-61 period averaged 22.5 per cent of GNP; Norway 29.6 per cent; the Netherlands, 22.6 per cent; Sweden, 20.9 per cent; France, 18.3 per cent; Italy, 21.2 per cent; Austria, 21.2 per cent; and Spain, 18.3 per cent.[9]

Table 5 shows the distribution of private investment among the various sectors of the economy. These statistics reveal that the housing sector has been the leading contributor to Greece's economic growth, increasing its share of total private investment from 33.8 per cent in 1949-52 to 51.0 per cent in 1953-56, followed by a drop to 42.4 per cent in 1957-60 and a rise to 45.3 in the last four years. According to the latest statistics, investment activity in the housing sector in 1965 was somewhat reduced. As compared with other countries, Greece is clearly unique in that the housing sector absorbs a greater percentage of total investment than does any other single sector. Whereas in 1961 Greece devoted 31 per cent of gross capital formation to housing, Germany invested 21.9 per cent of its total investment to the same purpose; Portugal, 18.1 per cent; France, 22.3 per cent; Denmark, 21.7 per cent; Italy, 24.2 per cent; and the United Kingdom, 18.1 per cent.[10]

The impressively high rate of investment in the dwelling sector is explained partly by the need to meet the postwar housing shortage in Greece,[11] aggravated by the demographic changes that occurred over the period (the population increase, internal migration, and formation of new families), and partly by the limited opportunities for household savings to be invested in other financial assets. Psychological and social reasons must also be added to an explanation of the rapid annual rate of private

---

9. Organization for Economic Cooperation and Development, *Statistics of National Accounts,* Paris, 1963. These figures have been based on constant 1954 prices. The data for Spain cover the period 1954.
10. Ministry of Coordination, *National Accounts,* Vol. 13, Athens, 1964, p. 17.
11. The estimated accumulated housing deficit was about 670,000 dwelling units up to 1951, including extraordinary needs, dwelling construction to meet population increases, and new family fomation. See Ellis, Psilos, and Westebbe, *op. cit.*, p. 208.

investment in housing during the period under review. In addition to these stimulating factors, there should also be included the state housing policy after 1947-48, shaped by the prevalent shortage of housing, the widespread unemployment, and the government's decision to cut down the hoarding of gold sovereigns.

Table 5 shows that the contribution of the manufacturing and mining sectors to total private investment dropped from 32.7 per cent during the first period under review to 10.9 per cent during the years 1961 to 1964. During 1965-66, the level appears to have been 14.9 per cent. By way of comparison, manufacturing investment in Austria in 1961 amounted to 33.4 per cent of total investment; Germany, 32.2 per cent; the United Kingdom, 30.4 per cent; France, 27 per cent; Italy 26.9 per cent; and Portugal, 23.8 per cent.

Private investment in agriculture increased from 7.6 per cent of total private fixed capital formation during the 1949-52 period to 13.6 per cent in 1957-60, then declined to 11.9 per cent in 1960-62 and 9.7 per cent in 1963-64. In the last two years the trend has again reversed. The ratio of aggregate investment, both private and public, in Greek agriculture since 1957 is similar to that in developed countries as well as in those that are purely agricultural. France invested 7.9 per cent of its total fixed investment in agriculture during the 1957-59 period; Italy, 11.9 per cent; Austria, 13.4 per cent; and Portugal, 11.3 per cent, while the comparable figure for Greece was 14.7 per cent.[12] The high rate of investment in Greek agriculture over the whole period from 1957 to 1966 is partly due to increased participation of the national government in agricultural investment and to the increasingly larger volume of investment undertaken by local authorities in the rural areas. The increased governmental participation is explained by the desire to develop the agricultural sector through new methods of production and through land improvement.

The role of public investment over the entire period may be assessed by looking at the statistics recorded in Table 6. The

---

12. *National Accounts*, vol. 13, *op. cit.*, p. 13. These percentages are calculated at current prices.

Table 6: Distribution of Governmental Investment Expenditures,[a] 1949-64

	1949-52	1953-56	1957-60	1961-64	1949-64
Agriculture	17.9%	11.0%	19.0%	21.9%	18.9%
Manufacturing and mining	2.0	4.5	3.8	8.2	5.5
Electricity and water	10.2	31.4	21.9	22.0	21.3
Transportation and communications	33.7	17.3	34.0	35.1	32.0
Housing	15.6	17.4	9.2	2.9	8.7
Public administration	11.8	10.0	4.2	2.8	5.7
Other activities	8.8	8.4	7.9	7.1	7.9
TOTAL	100.0	100.0	100.0	100.0	100.0

[a]This has been calculated at constant prices except for the years 1963 and 1964, where current prices have been used.

Sources: Ministry of Coordination, *National Accounts*, Vol. 13 Athens, 1964; and Ministry of Coordination.

participation of the public sector in the total investment field declined from 40.9 per cent in 1949-52 to 29.9 per cent in 1963-64 and 25.5 per cent in 1965-66. The government investment policy favored primarily those sectors with high capital/output ratio. Nevertheless, both the volume and distribution of public investment over the period under review can be regarded as the most growth-stimulating actions of government. Total government investment outlays, calculated in constant prices, increased from a level of about 12 billion drachmas over the 1949-52 period to 30 billion drachmas in 1961-64, with total expenditure over the entire 1949-64 period coming to about 68 billion drachmas. (These figures also include related expenditures on public administration and other activities, which accounted for 13.6 per cent of total investment outlays over the entire 1949-64 period.)

About 13.0 billion drachmas or 18.9 per cent of total public investment over the 1949-64 period went into agriculture, primarily for land reclamation, flood protection, and irrigation, and for improved management, marketing and distribution facilities. All these forms of investment have contributed significantly to the growth in agriculture and thereby to the over-all economic growth of the economy.

Substantial government capital funds were also spent in the public utilities sectors, thus directly promoting productivity growth. Over the entire period investment in infrastructure—electric power, transport, and communications, and so forth—absorbed about 44 billion drachmas, or about 54 per cent of total public investment outlays up to 1965. All these are capital-intensive sectors, whose investment has been a substantial part of final demand and an important contribution to the growth of production potential. Investments in electric power production and water distribution were given high priority in the allocation of public funds, particularly in the years 1953 through 1956, when investment averaged about 31.4 per cent of total public investment outlays over this period. In the subsequent years this field continued to absorb large amounts of funds, averaging about 21.9 per cent of total government investment in 1957–60, and 22.0 per cent in 1961–64, reaching a level of 32 per cent once more in 1965. Transportation and communications followed an interesting cycle, declining from the peak of 48.2 per cent of total public investment in 1948 to an average of 33.7 per cent in 1949–52, and then to a minimum of 17.3 per cent in 1953–56, rising again to 34.0 per cent in 1957–60, 35.1 per cent in 1961–64, and 40 per cent in 1965.

Another interesting development in the public investment sector has been government expenditure on residential housing for workers and public employees. In the first three years of the period (1948–50), spending on housing averaged 27.9 per cent of total public investment; this declined to 7.7 per cent in 1951–52 but rose to 17.4 per cent in 1953–56. In subsequent years the share of residential housing sector to total public investment has declined considerably, reaching the very low level of 2.9 per cent in 1961–64. In 1965 public expenditure on housing increased to about 5 per cent of total public investment.

In short, the volume and composition of public investments assume great significance in the case of Greece, because they played a major role in building the basic infrastructure and creating a dynamic economy. All investment in road and bridge construction, in electric power and communications, as well as in the housing-construction sector, contributed directly to the development of the economy and gave the major stimulus to demand.

The impact of aggregate investment undertaken over the period under review upon Greece's economic growth may be evaluated by examining its relationship to total output. The estimated marginal fixed capital coefficients—that is, the amount of real fixed investment necessary to increase a unit of real gross national product—are given in Table 4. Marginal capital/output ratio for the economy as a whole declined from 3.16 to 2.47 between 1949 and 1956, to rise to 3.69 in the subsequent years.

The decline in the coefficient during the 1952–56 period may be explained partly by the impact of devaluation of the drachma and the liberalization of trade in 1953, which encouraged many enterprises in the manufacturing sector to import modern equipment. Meanwhile, other sectors required relatively little investment expenditure to restore to production certain enterprises only partially damaged by the war and guerrilla warfare or underutilized up to 1952. Furthermore, the structure of investment during the first period under review favored industries such as transportation and communication, harbors, irrigation projects etc., whose full effect on the economy was not felt until after 1952.

The increase in the marginal capital coefficient for the economy as a whole from 1957 on may be explained partly by the substitution of capital for labor that took place in some sectors, because of wage increases and shortage of labor (in agriculture, mining, and other sectors) and partly by structural factors in the investment sector itself. Thus, the pattern of investment after 1957 influenced unfavorably the productivity of gross investment. Large capital-intensive projects were undertaken in transportation, communication, hospitals, schools, housing, and other areas, all of which account for the greater capital requirements and higher capital coefficients observed since 1957. Tables 4, 5, and 6 present the change in the relative share to total gross investment of all main sectors throughout the entire period from 1949 to 1964.

Not all industries experienced a decline in their investment productivity. The housing and energy sectors had an average marginal capital-output ratio of 10.85 and 9.5 respectively over the entire period. Manufacturing showed an over-all improvement in capital-output ratios; its marginal fixed investment coefficient was 2.77 in 1949–52, 1.23 in 1953–56, 1.79 in 1957–60, and 1.60 in 1959–62. Agriculture's capital coefficient rose and then fell again;

it was .83 in 1948-51, 1.14 in 1954-57, 6.45 in 1956-59 and 1.76 in 1960-62.[13]

The capital coefficients in manufacturing and agriculture declined as a result of innovations in technology and organization. This was especially true in the paper industry, in electric appliances, in basic metals and metal manufacturers and chemicals. In agriculture there was considerable mechanization as well as improved farming methods, introduction of better seeds, improved irrigation conditions, and increased use of fertilizers.

The qualitative improvement in capital stock is clearly seen in the composition of imports, which shows that most industrial equipment installed in Greece since 1954 has been recorded as "imported." As a result a good deal of new technological skill developed in the advanced industrial economies has been embodied in these imports.[14] Other factors leading to the considerable improvement of domestic skills and the state of technology have included the rising standard of general education and the establishment of new technical schools since the war, the reallocation of resources from less to more efficient enterprises within the manufacturing sector, and the realization of external economies due to improvements in the infrastructure over the period under review. All this has contributed much to increases in industrial output since 1951, the quantitative coefficient being estimated by Archibald to be around 3.89 per cent out of about 7.0 per cent increase in industrial output over the decade 1951-61. Similarly, technical progress in Greek agriculture may be seen in the changes that have occurred in the input combinations since 1950 in the production of this sector.[15]

	1950	1962
Machinery (units per 1000 hectares)	2.2	6.4
Use of fertilizers (kilograms per hectares)	15.0	43.0
Labor (wages per hectare)	52.0	58.0
Farm Income ($ per hectare in 1954 prices)	100.0	156.0

---

13. Account has been taken of the two-year cycle regularly observed in the olive-oil production. *National Accounts*, Vol. 13, *op. cit.*, pp. 31-33.
14. See G. C. Archibald, *Investment and Technical Change in Greek Manufacturing*, Lecture Series, No. 15 (Athens: Center of Economic Research, 1964), pp. 40-41.
15. George Coutsoumaris, Richard Westebbe, and Diomedes D. Psilos, *Analysis and Assessment of the Economic Effects of the U.S. PL 480 Program in Greece* (Athens: Center of Economic Research, forthcoming), p. IV-7.

Thus, the rise in agricultural production resulted primarily from the considerable increase in the use of capital inputs in the form of machinery and fertilizers. Furthermore, about $383 million were invested by the government in land improvements, irrigation works, and other social overheads in agriculture, throughout the postwar period, as compared with about $700 million of total investment in this sector over the same period.

In addition to the registered technical progress over the period, most firms have reduced or eliminated their excess capacity in the course of the last decade. It is common to view the industrial sector in Greece as having substantial excess capacity.[16] Both Coutsoumaris and the Federation of Greek Industrialists independently report substantial excess capacity in manufacturing, but this apparently exists in all nonagricultural producing units. This surplus capacity has been unquestionably reduced over the 1950-65 period. Thus, the one-shift basis of production was replaced by a multiple-shift scheme whenever a greater supply of output could be economically marketed; in some cases quasi-monopolistic positions were abandoned because of higher aggregate profits earned through mass-production. Hence, the Greek entrepreneurs had some scope for growth without new investment, particularly over short-term periods.

The Role of Foreign Trade

Due to its small size and the existing structural defects in its economy, Greece's productivity and economic growth are closely tied to the volume and pattern of foreign trade. Indeed, the main constraint on growth in the past has been the volume and pattern of Greece's international transactions, a fact that

---

16. George Coutsoumaris, *The Morphology of Greek Industry* (Athens: Center of Economic Research, 1963), pp. 304-305; and *Annual Reports* of the Federation of Greek Industries.

poses policy problems for present and also future policy makers. This section analyzes the significance of this constraint and reviews the government's commercial and foreign exchange policies that seem to have influenced the rate of economic growth.

Trends in Exports and Imports

Greece's trade deficit has been growing since 1948. In absolute terms, it increased from $290 million in 1948 to $324 million in 1951, declining to $112 million in 1953. From then on, as shown in Table 7, the deficit in the balance of trade has increased at an annual rate of 13.6 per cent, rising in absolute terms from $161.5 million in 1954 to $745.4 million in 1966. In relation to exports, the trade deficit during the 1948–51 period was more than three times greater than exports, or to put it more pre-

Table 7: Imports, Exports, and Balance of Trade, 1954-66
(in millions of U. S. dollars)

Period	Imports Volume (1)	% of GNP (2)	Exports Volume (3)	% of GNP (4)	Balance of Trade Volume (5)	% of Exports (Col 3) (6)
1954	$321.2	18.8%	$159.7	9.1%	$-161.5	1.01%
1955	383.2	19.4	206.5	10.5	-177.7	.86
1956	476.5	20.6	209.6	9.1	-266.9	1.27
1957	530.3	21.4	222.9	9.0	-307.4	1.35
1958	542.0	21.1	243.1	9.4	-298.9	1.23
1959	470.2	17.5	212.5	7.9	-257.7	1.21
1960	520.4	14.6	208.4	7.3	-312.0	1.49
1961	567.2	13.5	234.3	5.6	-332.9	1.42
1962	640.3	14.3	242.6	5.4	-397.7	1.64
1963	731.6	14.8	295.9	6.0	-435.7	1.47
1964	863.4	15.3	308.4	5.5	-555.0	1.80
1965	1,016.5	15.9	330.9	5.2	-685.6	2.07
1966	1,148.9	16.3	403.5	5.7	-745.4	1.85
Annual compound rate of change, 1954-66	11.2%	—	8.0%	—	13.6%	—

Sources: Bank of Greece; Ministry of Commerce; and American Embassy, Athens.

cisely, the ratio of trade balance to exports was 3.35 during those years. Since then, however, this ratio has ranged from 8.6 to 2.07.

While exports have increased at an annual compound rate of 8.0 per cent since 1954, imports have increased at a rate of 11.2 per cent. In absolute terms, imports rose from $321 million in 1954 to $1,149 million in 1966, whereas exports rose only from $160 million to $404 million over the same period.

Expressed as a ratio to GNP, imports declined from a range of about 20 percent over the period up to 1958 to 13.5 per cent in 1961, then rose again to 16.3 per cent in 1966. But the ratio of exports to GNP has declined almost without interruption from 10.5 per cent in 1955, to 5.2 in 1965, and 5.7 in 1966.

The rising volume of foreign trade has undoubtedly been a stimulus to economic development in Greece, in fostering both productivity and high levels of demand. Of course, this stimulus would have been much stronger if imports had not been increasing faster than exports; nevertheless, both exports and imports have positively influenced the rate of productivity and growth.

In the field of exports, cotton, citrus fruit, and other new industries were developed, while the traditional export commodities, such as tobacco, olive oil, wine, and figs, had somewhat exceeded prewar production levels by the end of 1953. These developments reflect both structural changes in agricultural production and increased foreign demand, especially a demand for fruit and vegetables from the Eastern Bloc under bilateral trade agreements. Notwithstanding, however, this increased demand for traditional as well as new export commodities, the problem of Greece's exports is very acute: the agricultural export industry is adversely influenced by weather conditions and strong international competition, while the exporting capacity of the manufacturing sector is very low and oriented toward a protected domestic market.

As for imports, it must be noted that their relatively rapid rise up to 1958 was mainly due to the progressive liberation of certain nonessential imports from direct controls; this action was taken with a view to keeping down domestic price rises that were anticipated because of the devaluation of 1953. Likewise,

Table 8: Selected Imports[a] (Index: 1953 =

Commodity categories	1954	1955	195
Livestock, fishery products	112.4	155.8	20(
Agricultural products, foods and beverages	92.0	133.2	17:
Hides, skins, etc.	170.0	156.8	16
Mineral materials (metallic and nonmetallic)	118.7	136.1	13
Metals and metal articles	151.2	171.8	21(
Chemical and pharmaceutical products	214.0	201.8	22
Paper and paper products	165.0	174.7	21(
Textiles	163.8	159.8	17
Miscellaneous	164.2	187.4	22:
Total	140.5	160.7	19(

[a]Excludes ships.
Source: Ministry of Coordination, *Foreign Trade of Greece, 1953-1963.*

Table 9: Imports by Major Categories (percent

	1955	1956	1957	195
1. Foodstuffs	20.1	27.5	19.4	1
2. Raw materials	21.6	20.5	27.3	2
3. Fuels-lubricants	12.4	10.7	12.6	
4. Capital goods	12.8	14.3	11.1	1
5. Industrial consumption goods	28.5	23.7	27.2	2
6. Freight charges	4.6	3.3	2.4	
Total[a]	100.0	100.0	100.0	10(

[a]Details may not add to totals due to rounding.
Source: Bank of Greece, *Annual Reports.*

57	1958	1959	1960	1961	1962	1963
9.1	207.8	186.3	189.7	234.1	222.2	263.8
5.8	139.4	115.5	114.8	140.4	108.4	161.9
4.9	202.8	179.1	220.0	210.5	212.7	256.4
2.8	157.9	132.2	142.5	140.8	142.1	198.9
3.4	305.7	292.7	348.6	429.5	509.7	524.9
4.4	332.5	310.5	339.3	369.1	426.0	516.2
7.8	240.7	232.6	234.2	261.3	268.2	332.7
4.6	203.3	161.9	208.1	202.0	206.3	249.9
7.8	295.5	276.0	263.7	281.9	330.2	386.8
7.7	228.2	205.5	223.4	250.9	271.5	319.5

59	1960	1961	1962	1963	1964	1965	1966
5.6	18.8	17.8	14.0	18.6	16.8	18.1	16.4
5.5	26.5	25.1	24.9	23.4	24.0	22.0	21.9
1.3	9.6	8.4	7.9	7.3	6.7	6.9	7.0
8.2	15.7	17.8	22.3	18.9	21.7	23.5	22.6
9.1	29.4	30.9	30.9	31.6	30.0	28.2	31.0
0.3	—	—	—	0.2	0.9	1.4	1.2
0.0	100.0	100.0	100.0	100.0	100.0	100.0	100.0

the continuous large increases in imports since 1958 can also be explained by government commercial policy.

The changing composition of imports since the mid-1950's can be seen in Tables 8 and 9.

Table 8 shows that imports of metals and metal articles have risen by an average annual rate of about 42.5 per cent since 1953, chemical and pharmaceutical products by about 41.6 per cent, paper and paper articles by 23.3 per cent, livestock and fishery products by 16.4 per cent, and hides and skins by 15.6 per cent. Table 9 indicates that the Greek economy imported large quantities of capital goods and raw materials to supply the process of economic development, and also of manufactured consumption goods and foodstuffs to demand arising from the increase in money incomes. On the assumption that the over-all balance of payments remained sound, this rise in imports could not but stimulate the growth of the Greek economy, since it put the industrial sector on a higher technological plane and "created a market for products which will soon reach a size sufficient to justify the production of import substitutes."[17]

Commercial Policy, 1953-1966. The turning point in Greece's commercial policy was the devaluation of the drachma in April 1953, which reduced the value of the drachma, in terms of the United States dollar from one-to-fifteen to one-to-thirty. Until then, the increasing overvaluation of the drachma was disguised by large subsidies, by tight credit, and by a system of import controls designed to preserve scarce foreign exchange. In 1953, all of these import and exchange controls were relaxed, except for the customs duties.

Through the devaluation of the drachma and the liberalization of trade after 1953, many Greek products regained a competitive position. Indeed, exports of the traditional agricultural products, which account for more than 75 per cent of total exports, increased substantially from 2,476 million drachmas in 1953 to 4,892 million drachmas in 1958, rising at a rate of 14.6 per cent a year. Since 1958, agricultural exports have fluctuated at much lower levels. Imports, on the other hand, more than

---

17. Coutsoumaris, Westebbe, Psilos, *op. cit.*, p. IX-3.

doubled, rising from 6,904 million drachmas in 1953 to 15,756 million drachmas in 1958, or at a rate of 18.0 per cent annually— an increase that cannot be entirely explained by increases in real per capita income in Greece. This rise in imports declined somewhat during the following three years and increased rapidly after 1961 at a rate of 14.2 per cent a year.

However, in order to achieve the most desirable composition of imports from the point of view of industrialization and to assure domestic monetary stability, the Greek government began imposing various import restraints. Introduced in 1954 and 1955, these included quantitative as well as qualitative regulations for the banking system in granting credits to the foreign trade sector; shorter time limits on customs clearance; advance deposits against bills of lading, covering between 15 and 100 per cent of the value of imported goods, etc.[18] These measures were quite effective in preventing the importation of large quantities of luxuries and other nonessential commodities over the years 1955 and 1956.

In the latter part of 1956 some of these measures were relaxed, only to be reimposed again in 1958. In that year an additional measure was adopted for the purpose of retarding consumption of nonessential commodities: consumer sales taxes were levied on nonessential imported and domestic goods, and the tax for licensing passenger cars was substantially raised. In 1959 the worsening trade deficit brought about the imposition of import quotas on certain products not directly contributing to economic growth, and special licenses were required for the importation of various consumer durables. The imports of these goods declined immediately, leading to substantial savings in foreign exchange.[19]

In 1960 import quotas were eliminated, and in subsequent years a more liberal foreign trade policy was adopted. For example, the time limit for settling payments under foreign sup-

---

18. For a more detailed analysis of these measures see *Reports of the Governor of the Bank of Greece,* for the years 1954, 1955 and 1956; and also X. Zolotas, *Monetary Equilibrium and Economic Development* (New Jersey: Princeton University Press, 1965), pp. 134-140.
19. X. Zolotas, *op. cit.*, p. 135.

pliers' credit was extended from 6 to 12 months for all commodities, and in the case of imported mechanical equipment and spare parts the limit was increased to three years. Furthermore, the association of Greece with the European Common Market in November 1962 brought about tariff cuts—a 5 per cent cut in tariffs on imports from the EEC countries, for goods that are also manufactured locally, and for a 10 per cent cut on those goods not produced in Greece. In May 1964 there was another 10 per cent reduction of duties on EEC imports not manufactured in Greece, and a still further 10 per cent cut went into effect in November 1965. A reduction of advance deposits required for some imported articles also was introduced, and this was extended to goods imported from non-Common Market countries. During the first four years of its association with the EEC, Greece reduced tariffs by 30 per cent on industrial and agricultural products. This has had an important impact on Greek development. Whereas in 1960-62 agricultural exports financed 46.7 per cent of manufactured consumption goods imports, in the year 1965 the figure rose to 52.6 per cent.[20]

In short, commercial policy since 1955 has been designed so as to maintain total imports within limits that would not endanger the country's external equilibrium and at the same time to bring about significant shifts in the composition of imports in favor of goods for investment purpose.[21] However, in spite of rising exports, the fact remains that both domestic and external equilibrium would not have been achieved if the trade balance was not substantially covered by "invisible resources" and other capital inflows.

Throughout the postwar period, the account of invisibles has risen drastically, especially since the restoration of monetary stability in 1956. Emigrant remittances financed about 48 per cent of the trade deficit over the 1957-63 period and 32 per cent in 1963-66, while 42 per cent was financed by shipping remittances and tourist's foreign exchange receipts in 1957-63 and 43 per cent in 1963-66.*

---

20. Bank of Greece, *Report for 1965*, p. 71.
21. X. Zolotas, *op. cit.*, pp. 136-137.
*See Memorandum by CHARLES P. KINDLEBERGER, p. 69.

The remaining current deficit has been covered by:

- *United States grant aid*, (including PL 480 and PL 665 aid, as well as technical assistance), all forms of which contributed 19 per cent to the deficit on current account in 1957, 23.4 per cent in 1958, 60.8 in 1959, 36.5 in 1960, 40.4 in 1961, 16 in 1962, 37.8 in 1963, 8 in 1964 and 1 per cent in 1965.
- *Net lending from abroad,* which has financed about 15 per cent of total current deficit since 1957.
- *Suppliers' credit*, which financed about 16 per cent of total current account deficit over the period 1957-63 and 17 per cent in 1965-66.
- *Direct foreign investment in Greece,* amounting to $84.1 million up to 1963, and to about $160 million over the period 1964-1966.
- *Other private capital inflows,* including repatriated capital from Greeks living abroad other than emigrant remittances, which amounted to about $300 million up to 1963 and to $175 million over the last three years. Although most of this capital was invested in housing and real estate, it must be admitted that it led to substantial increases in the foreign exchange reserves of the country, financing thus a corresponding volume of imports, contributing thereby to the maintenance of the relatively high rate of growth which the Greek economy experienced in the last decade.
- *Official gold and short-term capital items,* such as gold and convertible assets which increased over most of the recent years. Over the 1954-63 period, gold and convertible assets rose by $224 million, while during the 1964-1965 period these reserves increased by $21 million a year.

Notwithstanding the significant rise in the foreign exchange reserves, however, Greece's balance of payments contains structural weaknesses that render the country's foreign trade position very vulnerable. Apart from the limited export capacity of the economy, the high import-income elasticity of the Greek population causes the balance of payments to be dependent on invisible sources of foreign exchange and upon other private government capital inflows.

Conclusions Regarding the Role of Foreign Trade. The foregoing analysis indicates that the future rate of growth of the Greek economy will depend, as it has in the past, on the pattern and volume of foreign trade. There are three reasons why this is likely to be so.

First, under conditions of a flexible government trade policy, the foreign trade component of gross national product historically has represented an "inevitable accompaniment of economic development and rising incomes."[22]

For Greece in particular, both exports and imports have played a decisive role in the past and are also expected to be important variables in the future. The rising real income per capita will induce a high propensity to import, which in turn will lead to more investment in export industries,[23] as well as to the absorption of whatever excess capacity exists in some of them. Thus imports will remain an important stimulant for more exports, although government should, through special incentives, favor investment in import substitute industries as well.

Second, the small size of the country will continue to tie Greece's economic growth to the foreign sector, with the result that ". . . an increment in per capita income of given magnitude will necessitate more imports and exports, and more investment for exports, than for a large country."[24] Hence, bound by her size Greece will continue to face balance-of-payments problems as growth proceeds.

Third, Greece has linked its development with the eco-

---

22. Ellis, Psilos, and Westebbe, *op. cit.*, pp. 24–25.
23. This implies that the higher propensity to import will positively influence the export industries. *First*, by the fact that some export industries—metal, mines, chemicals etc.—are highly capital-intensive industries supported by a great deal of imported foreign technology. *Second*, unless the country is prepared to see its foreign exchange reserves decline, it must take drastic measures to develop export industries in order to balance the added imports. *Third*, other things being equal, a higher propensity to import will lead to a fall in prices, stimulating foreign demand for Greek products. And *last*, assuming that the increased imports will satisfy domestic demand in some fields, a shift of resources should be expected into export industries. In addition, one may say that the orientation of Greece's imports toward the Common Market countries is expected to lead to somewhat higher demand for its products and services on the part of these countries.
24. Ellis, Psilos, and Westebbe, *op. cit.*, p. 25.

nomic growth of the advanced economies of the Common Market countries of Europe, and both the volume and pattern of Greece's foreign trade has to change drastically on the basis of the rules of adjustment that Greece has to follow. Some of these rules of adjustment are required by the Athens Treaty, but certain others stem from the severe competition to Greek industry and agriculture from the European economies.

Foreign Aid as a Factor in Greece's Economic Growth

World War II and the Civil War that grew out of it wiped out most of the prewar real and financial resources of Greece. Productive efficiency in agriculture and manufacturing was brought to a lower level than ever before. Hyperinflation put the economy virtually on a barter basis through 1946, destroying all confidence in the currency. Communications were thrown into a state of almost complete chaos. More than 25 per cent of all buildings were destroyed, and this together with other destruction constituted an over-all loss of capital stock of about $8.5 billion. At the end of the Civil War, which lasted until 1949, nearly a tenth of the population was awaiting resettlement in devastated villages, while a third of the population was either wholly or partially dependent on state aid.[25] As can readily be understood, economic progress in Greece during this period had to depend to a great extent upon foreign economic, technical, and military assistance.

The influence of foreign aid on Greece's economic growth varies in each of several major postwar periods, according to both domestic and international developments.

---
25. A. G. Papandreou, *op. cit.*, Ch. I.

The Period Prior to the Truman Doctrine

The first period—1944 to 1947—is distinguished from the other periods by the humanitarian concern of all Western countries over the socio-economic and political survival of Greece. Almost all aid up to 1947 was given to Greece through emergency multilateral aid programs, and priority was given at the beginning mainly to foodstuffs and medicines. Whatever bilateral aid was given to Greece was largely of military type in order to meet the Communist aggression and came principally from the United Kingdom.

Up to 1947, the United Nations Relief and Rehabilitation Administration's (UNRRA) essential supplies and services represented the main form of economic and technical assistance to Greece. This form of aid amounted to $416 million, of which $312 million was provided by the United States, the remaining $104 million being supplied by the other allies of Greece.[26] UNRRA supplies consisted of essential foodstuffs, medicines, and emergency repair works, including road and bridge construction.

Over the same period, Great Britain granted to Greece a total of $152 million in terms of military aid. In addition, indirect aid was given through UNRRA over the 1944–47 period. Another $135.2 million was extended to Greece over the same period by Great Britain, of which $56 million represented the Bank of Greece's sterling exchange resources expendable in the sterling area, while $49.2 million was in the form of British Military Authority notes issued in Greece and advanced in drachmas by the Central Bank to British military forces. To the above foreign grants should be added $14.6 million United States assistance extended through the Export-Import Bank in 1946.

As was indicated above, the main characteristic of foreign aid given to Greece over the period 1944–47 was its "emergency basis," which meant the absence of well-defined foreign aid programs on the part of all involved; that is both the donor coun-

---

26. See Diomedes D. Psilos, and Richard Westebbe, *Public International Development Financing in Greece*, (New York: Columbia University School of Law, September 1964), p. 14.

tries and Greece put little or no emphasis on long-term development of the Greek economy. Military and political considerations dominated this international assistance, which was focused mainly on the elimination of foreign Communist influence over Greece.

Notwithstanding these noneconomic considerations, however, and regardless of the composition of aid, the fact remains that over the first three postwar years Greece's economy was favorably influenced by these capital inflows. In the first place, UNRRA supplies checked the price rises set in motion during the first postwar months. The increase in prices resumed following the discontinuation of UNRRA imports after June 1947. The first foodstuffs and medical supplies imported through UNRRA into Greece immediately after Liberation Day prevented the Greek population from actual starvation, while the first quantities of machinery, equipment, and draft animals unquestionably laid the foundation for the subsequent reconstruction and rehabilitation plans that led the Greek economy to higher growth levels. Had the guerrilla war not occurred, the effects of foreign aid during the pre-Marshall Plan period would have been much stronger and longer lasting.

Foreign Aid During 1947-1954

The termination of UNRRA's emergency aid marks the beginning of the United States foreign aid program in Greece, characterized by its long-term economic and diplomatic objectives. On March 3, 1947, the Greek Prime Minister made a dramatic plea for help to the President of the United States; this followed Great Britain's urgent message to the United States stating most emphatically that the British government would be unable to provide any further economic and military assistance to Greece after March 31, 1947. President Truman thereupon requested Congress on March 12 to appropriate a grant of $350 million to Greece to finance imports of foodstuffs and other essentials, including capital equipment for reconstruction, and military expenditures.

The American people took a favorable view of Truman's

request, and $300 million was approved by Congress, $150 million being earmarked for reconstruction and stabilization, the remaining $150 for military expenditures. However, guerrilla warfare developments during the second half of 1947 led to a reconsideration of the use of these aid resources, resulting in a heavy emphasis on military programs. The rapidly changing political events in 1947 led to the adoption of a completely elastic aid program, both on the part of the Greek government as well as on the part of the American Mission for Aid to Greece, in the sense that funds were distributed among economic and military uses without any clear ideas as to the actual conditions prevailing at the time.

The various inflows of capital over the period from 1947 to 1954 are shown in Table 10.

Table 10 shows that foreign aid of the type that is generally believed to have positively contributed to economic growth in Greece amounted to $1,409.9 million over the first eight years of the postwar reconstruction period. This represents about 60 per cent of the over-all public development capital inflows into Greece up to the end of 1962, which indicates once again that the bases for economic growth in Greece's economy were built over the 1948–54 period. Most of this capital flow came from the United States in the form of grants. Only $5.7 million came from Canada, while $110.7 million came from Germany and Italy in the form of war reparations over the

Table 10: Inflows of Capital to Greece, 1947-54
(in millions of U. S. dollars)

	1947/48	1948/49	1949/50	1950/51	1951/52	1952/53	1953/54
Economic aid[a]	$197.1	$243.9	$288.5	$285.0	$181.1	$ 81.2	$ 22.4
Reparations	—	5.7	24.9	32.9	28.2	11.9	7.1
Total Development Aid	197.1	249.6	313.4	317.9	209.3	93.1	29.5
Military aid	189.4	158.7	22.5	83.0	59.3	121.3	95.2
GRAND TOTAL	386.5	408.3	335.9	400.9	268.6	214.4	124.7

[a]Includes technical assistance.
Source: Bank of Greece.

1947-54 period. To this economic and technical assistance, should be added an amount of $729.4 million used for military purposes. This represented 46 per cent of total military aid granted throughout the postwar period.

The main characteristic of the period under review (1947-54) is that the annual United States assistance inflows started declining rapidly after 1952, while the first positive effects of the earlier aid programs manifested themselves after that year. Indeed, after 1952 gross national product rose much faster than before, and domestic savings financed a greater percentage of gross investment. Meanwhile, the restoration of government stability made possible the better allocation and utilization of whatever aid was given, spurring the growth of the key sectors of the economy and lessening the unfavorable balance of trade.

There was a considerable reduction in American economic and technical assistance after 1952—from $179.9 million in 1951/52, to $81.2 in 1952/53, to $21.9 million in 1953/54. This led to a shift in Greek government policy with respect both to individual foreign sources of capital and to Greek imports. Greek officials adopted the view that the financing of economic development must take place mainly from within and that where foreign capital might be needed, it must be sought on the European markets; as for imports, they must once again be oriented toward European Payments Union (EPU) countries.[27] At the same time, rigid exchange-restriction policies were applied. Under such conditions, imports of capital and consumer goods fell considerably in absolute terms, declining from $449.2 million in 1948/49 to $351.9 million in 1951/52 and to $230.1 million in 1952/53. Furthermore, the decline in United States economic aid after 1952 is partly explained by the new foreign aid policy embodied in the Mutual Security Act of 1951 and partly by the effective economic and institutional measures adopted by the Greek government in 1951 and 1952, designed to balance the budget and to bring the long-term development program more in line with the financial and technological capacity of the Greek economic system.

---

27. See Psilos and Westebbe, *op. cit.*, p. 23.

Foreign long-term economic assistance in Greece over the period 1949-54 was used mainly for the purpose of economic development, including land reclamation, agriculture, food processing, power projects, manufacturing, and mining. Such distribution of aid funds aimed at restoring the production of foodstuffs and of traditional agricultural exports; enlarging the country's social overhead capacity (especially communications, transformation, electric power); and financing imports of essential items, capital goods, and raw materials. The last of these three uses of foreign aid assumed a greater significance over the period under review, for the inflationary pressures and the dislocation of the industrial sector up to 1949 had wiped out almost all foreign reserves availabilities of the country.

The foreign aid funds appropriated for industrial development were made available to individual firms through the so-called Central Loan Committee (CLC), established in November 1948 with the participation of the United States Economic Cooperation Administration (ECA) Mission. (ECA had veto power over each loan decision.) Over the entire period of its operation (1948-54), CLC loaned a total of $80.5 million, of which 52.4 per cent went to manufacturing, 14.7 per cent to agriculture and fishing, 13.4 per cent to mining, 12.4 per cent to power, 5.4 per cent to communications and transportation, and 1.7 per cent to tourism. It should be noted that all loans granted by CLC were to be repaid in dollars, at the prevailing rate of exchange at the time of repayment, and their maturity varied, ranging from 5 to 20 years according to the activity and sector financed.

Foreign Aid Programs, 1954-1963

Both the sources and types of foreign aid have changed significantly since 1954, reflecting new economic and political developments in the donor countries as well as in Greece. Thus, the United States Congress from 1954 onward has put more emphasis on the developmental character and use of international capital flows, taking into account not only the need for capital in developing countries but also the need at home for preserving economic stability and promoting economic growth. Similar considerations were present as France, Great Britain, and West Germany launched programs to penetrate developing areas of the world.

In the case of Greece, the United States Congress under the International Cooperation Administration (ICA) program, which commenced in 1954-55, did not authorize any "development assistance" per se for Greece, but only Defense Support Aid, the drachma counterpart of which was used to provide funds to finance the construction and expansion of approved projects in the budget. This defense support program meant, for Greece, an annual amount of about $40 or $50 million up to 1959-60 and $20 million for the two final years (1961 and 1962) of the program.

Similarly, under the Agricultural Trade Development and Assistance Acts (PL 480) of 1954, Greece received surplus agricultural commodities that amounted to $226.8 million over the 1954-63 period. Of this total commodity assistance, $109.3 million (including transportation cost) was provided under Title I, $3.8 million under Title II, and $113.7 million under Title III.

One of the most important aspects of the Title I program has been Section 104g loans to the Greek government for economic development. The total amount of these loans during the 1952-62 period was $52.5 million, which directly contributed to covering the deficit in the annual investment budgets over the same period. Three of these loans were granted for a maturity of 40 years, the remaining four loans for a maturity of 30 years; the interest rates were set at 4 per cent, with the exception of the 1958 $9.9 million loan, which was charged with a 5 per cent interest rate annually.

Besides the aforementioned loans, another $35 million was appropriated for Greece under Section 402 of PL 665. These were 40-year, 4 per cent loans (granted in 1955, 1956, and 1957) to serve the same purpose as the PL 480 loans: to aid the investment program of the Greek government.

In 1961 the new Administration in Washington effected sweeping changes in the over-all foreign aid program, resulting in better administration, coordination, and allocation of economic assistance. The development assistance to be granted to a large number of underdeveloped economies throughout the decade 1960-70 was put under the administration of a single agency, the Agency for International Development (AID), under which were combined the functions of ICA, Development Loan Fund (DLF), and other agencies, excluding the Export-Import Bank.

The main objective of the new agency was long-range planning in making United States funds available to developing economies of the free world. The primary instrument of this new agency was the long-term development loan authority, permitting loans at little or no interest with repayment in dollars. The previous "defense support" aid programs were to be reduced and terminated as soon as "countries prepare and begin sound programs for economic growth" that can be assisted by development lending.[28]

Under this new aid program, Greece was considered to be a country that could finance its economic development mainly through domestic sources, with some help from international loans. In 1961-62 Greece was given a last $20 million grant of supporting assistance with the clear warning that this would be the final such grant.

The new attitude toward Greece caused an unfavorable reaction in Greek academic and political circles. It was the general belief in Athens that grant aid was necessary for easing budgetary deficits and that a transition period of two to three years was needed in order to develop an effective machinery capable of producing a sufficient number of justifiable projects for international development loans and of coordinating and supervising the use of such loans.[29]

There were good grounds for this point of view. In 1958 there had been a DLF loan of $12 million to finance an import-substitute fertilizer factory that was found by feasibility reports to have been planned and executed with enormous errors and

---

28. Psilos and Westebbe, *op. cit.*, p. 32.
29. See "Doubts on Greece's Ability to Participate in American Development Lending Program," *Athens Daily Post*, November 30, 1961, front page.

technical difficulties.[30] To this example should be added the Acheloos Power Dam loan of $31 million in 1960, which was not utilized at all, while an application of the Agricultural Bank for $15 million to finance a variety of agricultural industries was later rejected by AID on the grounds that there was no adequate technical and economic justification for application.

One instance was an exception. AID approved a $20 million loan to the rapidly expanding Public Power Corporation to cover construction costs, in foreign exchange, of the hydroelectric units at Kastraki (Acheloos), which had been submitted well before the AID legislation came into being. But aside from this one exception, the Greek government was never able to produce sufficiently detailed development projects to meet the aid criteria of the new United States agency.

Recognizing these difficulties, the United States government took the initiative early in 1962 in forming the European Consortium to provide long-term financing to Greece. In the summer of 1962, all of the Organization for Economic Cooperation and Development (OECD) members, excluding the United Kingdom, established the Consortium, which granted to Greece $35 million to finance investment budget deficits and meet balance of payments difficulties. In July 1963, the United States also made available through the Consortium a $10 million, 2 per cent, 20-year loan to finance the import of essential development commodities from the United States. Similarly, France agreed in 1964 to make available $25 million for the procurement of commodities in France; Italy agreed to grant to the Greek government a $6 million, 6 per cent, 15-year loan to finance commodities imports from Italy; and Canada offered to make a $2 million loan at 6 per cent for 15 years to pay the foreign exchange costs for capital goods imported from Canada.

In addition to the above capital inflows, West Germany supplied Greece with long-term capital in terms of development loans and special long-term credits to public enterprises quite

---

30. Instead of costing $40 million as planned, the actual amount of capital needed to implement the project will be more than $65 million in excess of what the original planners had estimated, mainly because of rail and electric transmission lines needed.

independently from the Consortium. A loan in the amount of $48.2 million to the Greek government and another $13.9 million of special credits came into Greece over the period 1956-63. Much of these capital inflows were used for financing investment in agriculture, power, communications, and transportation over the period 1959-62. Further, in 1960, a loan was granted by West Germany to finance the construction of a sugar plant, and still another loan was made to finance a thermal plant in the Megalopolis district. To all these should be added $29.6 million in reparations paid to Greece since 1956, $24.2 million of which was paid in 1962 to Nazi victims.

The volume and nature of foreign aid granted to Greece over the period 1954-63, from all sources, is presented in Table 11.

Table 11: Inflows of Foreign Aid, 1954-63[a] (in millions of U. S. dollars)

	1954	1955	1956	1957	1958	1959	1960	1961	1962	1963
Economic Grants	$24.5	$71.5	$62.1	$71.3	$76.7	$44.4	$46.3	$57.4	$48.3	$32.2
Loans & Credits	—	14.2	19.3	27.9	24.8	21.9	35.1	35.3	17.5	13.0
Reparations	4.8	—	.2	.4	.6	.9	.8	.9	13.6	—
Total Development Aid	29.3	85.7	81.6	99.6	102.1	67.2	82.2	93.6	79.4	45.2
Military Aid	95.2	59.2	95.6	74.6	156.8	100.0	132.2	52.1	10.0	—

a. Fiscal years.
Source: American Embassy, Athens; and the Research Department of the Bank of Greece.

Thus, over the 1954-63 period, development aid, including reparations, amounted to $765.9 million, as compared to $1,409.9 million received over the first reconstruction period of 1947-54. Military aid, on the other hand, amounted to $775.7 million over the second period as compared to $729.4 million military aid granted to Greece during the period 1947-54. The reduction observed in the rate and nature of development aid given to Greece reflects the higher rate of growth and the dependence of the Greek economy on domestic sources.

Recent Developments. Over the last three years (1964-1966), the nature of assistance from abroad differs significantly from that received during previous years. With the exception of war reparations and a negligible amount of multilateral grant aid, mainly representing donations, all the rest was in terms of loans. Thus, in 1964, the public sector, including public enterprises, received from foreign sources an amount of $105 million, of which only $33 million was in terms of various forms of assistance and donations, while $55 million represented loans repayable in dollars and $17 million loans repayable in drachmas. In 1965, the volume of foreign grants was reduced by about 50 per cent over the previous year, or in absolute figures it was reduced to $17 million. Loans in dollars amounted to $61 million and loans repayable in drachmas to only $4 million. Finally, available statistics for 1966 indicate that total loans from abroad, on behalf of the Greek government and a few public enterprises, amounted to $90 million.[31]

As far as individual sources of these loans are concerned, published statistics cover only the years 1964 and 1965. According to this information, private American banks granted an amount of $42.1 million to the Greek government over these two years, Export-Import Bank $5.0 million, AID $25.9 million, the European Investment Bank $13.8 million, and the Consortium $15.1 million, while PL 480 loans of $16.3 million and $19.5 million were received under credit arrangements with various foreign sources. United States sources therefore accounted for 73 per cent of total direct public loans from abroad, excluding the various types of credits. European markets seem to have been unable, if not unwilling, to contribute to the financial requirements of Greece. Consequently, the government has been seeking over the last three years to borrow funds on the United States capital market as a substitute to aid programs that have been reduced to negligible amounts.

Summary. The capital inflows into the Greek public sector are summarized in Table 12.

---

31. *Reports* of the Bank of Greece for 1966 and 1967.

44   POSTWAR ECONOMIC PROBLEMS IN GREECE

Table 12:   Total Inflows of Capital for the Public Sector in Greece, 1944–66
(in millions of U. S. dollars)

	Amount	Per Cent
Economic grant aid[a]	$2,283.8	76.1%
Loans and Credits	580.4	19.3
Reparations[b]	135.9	4.6
Total Development Aid	3,000.1	100.0
Military Assistance[b]	1,657.1	–
GRAND TOTAL	$4,657.2	–

a. Includes technical aid.
b. Excludes 1963–1966 period.
Source: United States Embassy; and the Bank of Greece.

Table 12 shows that Greece has received a considerable amount of foreign aid, totaling $4,657 million since World War II. About 64 per cent of this amount, or $3,000 million, was in the form of development aid such as grants, loans, and reparations. The latter were mostly given to Greece in terms of capital equipment used directly for producing other goods and services and represents only about 4.6 per cent of total development aid, as compared to 76.1 per cent of grants and 19.3 per cent of loans. Military assistance up to the end of 1962, on the other hand, accounted for about 36 per cent of total capital inflows into Greece or, in absolute terms, $1,657 million.

*The Contribution of Foreign Aid
to Greece's Economic Growth*

The large volume of foreign aid received by Greece has unquestionably influenced the rate of economic growth over the entire period 1947–64. Hence a discussion of these developments is in order.

Effects on the Balance of Payments. As indicated above, the balance-of-payments deficit represents a chronic weakness of the Greek economy. Up to the end of 1951, domestic production —especially that of export crops—was at very low levels. Further inflationary pressures and the negligible amounts of invisible resources of foreign exchange made Greece's current account depend almost exclusively on foreign aid. Thus, over the 1947-51 period, foreign aid funds amounted to $1,072 million, as compared with a $1,048 million deficit in the balance of payments before aid. In the 1952-54 period, total aid amounted to $251 million, as compared with a $170 million deficit in the balance of payments before aid, while in the 1955-63 period, the total aid averaged $42.9 million per annum, as compared with a $16.9 million annual deficit in the balance of payments before aid.

After the considerable reduction in United States aid in 1953, the trade balance deficit was financed mainly by foreign exchange obtained from invisible sources. Net receipts from shipping, tourism, and emigrant remittances increased at an annual rate of 27.2 per cent from 1953 to 1964, totaling $2,124 million for the entire period. Shipping remittances amounted to $735 million, tourist remittances to $509 million, and emigrant remittances to $879 million for the years 1963-64.

The large inflows of foreign exchange from invisible sources can be explained by several factors. The main reason, of course, has been the rapid development in the economies of the free world. Likewise, government policies in Greece have contributed to the rapid increase in invisible receipts, particularly through measures that led to the restoration of monetary stability; aided the expansion of tourism; encouraged registration under the Greek flag of vessels previously registered under the so-called "flags of convenience"; and fostered emigration to European labor markets.

After 1954 foreign aid assumes indeed a lesser importance for Greece's economic development, for the volume and type of aid funds were smaller and quite different from that received prior to 1954. We refer in particular to the PL 480 program and its composition, which had more effect upon agricultural productivity, and less upon the balance-of-payments position of Greece. In view of the small annual sales proceeds from agricultural surplus commodities, PL 480 only marginally affected the foreign exchange position of the country. Westebbe has estimated the over-all saving of foreign exchange, throughout the 1955-

63 period, to be at about $116.1 million or $11.8 million per annum. To the extent that it financed imports which would have been affected in any event, this amount has contributed somewhat to the improvement in Greece's foreign exchange position. In view of the fact that the United States government had a shortage of local currency throughout the period, only part of the Title I program represented net foreign exchange savings, namely that part which was in the form of grants. All other PL 480 imports were not foreign exchange saving. "In the long run only that part of the program which is represented by grants and which would have taken place even in the absence of PL 480 financing, can be defined as foreign exchange saving."[32]

Effects on Productivity. The foreign assistance received by Greece throughout the postwar period has undoubtedly influenced the rate of productivity in Greece in many ways.

In the first seven-year period, foreign aid was mainly used to finance investment in social-overhead and public utilities, both of which have led to the creation of external economies in the economy. Thus, up to 1952, public investment in communication and transportation absorbed about 37 per cent of foreign aid devoted to financing the government investment sector; public administration, 11.1 per cent; electricity and water, 9 per cent; and agriculture, 17 per cent. In the subsequent period, these trends were changed drastically, and foreign aid contributed much less to the financing of public investment. These infrastructure investments represent sectors whose capital/output ratio is relatively high in Greece (around 10/1), and direct addition to total output created by the foreign aid programs, especially up to 1953, may not be considered as very large. Indirectly, however, these investments have contributed considerably to the rise in productivity.

The contribution of the aid program since 1953, however, cannot be viewed as contributing very largely to productivity in the macro-economic sense. Agricultural productivity in many fields, such as wheat, barley, and corn, had already risen by 1953

---

32. See Coutsoumaris, Westebbe, and Psilos, *op. cit.*, p. XII-11.

to levels of 20 and 30 per cent above the 1933–38 levels, while in truck crops, productivity had increased nearly 50 per cent. Nevertheless, the effects of aid given by the United States to Greece after that year, through PL 665 and PL 480 programs, cannot altogether be neglected. In terms of specific sectors, United States assistance since 1954 has had an important impact on domestic production and productivity.

Although from the United States side, the objectives of the PL 480 program are well known, the Greek government has viewed Title I as a form of conditional aid, aimed at supplementing domestic production in basic foodstuffs and feed grains, hence helping balance-of-payments difficulties. For instance, wheat and flour supplies in the early period of the program (1955–58) represented about 50 per cent of the total wheat availabilities, as against 15 per cent for subsequent years. Similarly, commodity shipments under PL 665, Section 402, make up 73.5 per cent of the total in value terms. The same applies to oil, fats, and dairy products. With respect to seed oil, the purpose has been to also maintain olive oil domestic prices in times of production shortages. Title III, on the other hand, has not been related to any policy program except insofar as the limited development of school lunches is concerned. This program has recently expanded to cover 400,000 children in 1964 and an estimated 600,000 children in 1965.[33]

The size and the relative importance of the PL 480 and PL 665 programs are shown in Table 13.

Table 13 shows that the bulk of PL 480 assistance commenced in 1955, as against the $2.4 million granted to Greece in the 1952–54 period, mainly under food donation programs carried out by voluntary agencies. Similarly, PL 665, Section 402, operated over six years in the period 1955–63 and, of the total amount of $76.9 million, $73.4 million was given to Greece over the first three years of the period. This program consisted mainly of bread grains.

Imports of wheat and flour under this program took place

---

33. The section on the effects of the PL 480 program in Greece draws heavily upon Coutsoumaris, Westebbe, and Psilos, *op. cit.*, Chapters III, IV, and VII.

Table 13: U. S. Commodity Shipments to Greece Under PL 665 and PL 480
(in millions of U. S. dollars)

Year	PL 480	PL 665	Total
1952	$ .5	$ —	$ .5
1953	.1	—	.1
1954	1.8	—	1.8
1955	27.1	18.9	46.0
1956	28.2	29.4	57.6
1957	40.7	25.1	65.8
1958	40.4	1.4	41.8
1959	11.6	—	11.6
1960	13.5	1.1	14.6
1961	25.2	1.0	26.2
1962	19.1	—	19.1
1963	19.2	—	19.2
Total	$227.4	$76.9	$304.3

Source: Ministry of Commerce and Coordination;
and American Embassy, Athens.

at an average annual rate of 224,000 tons as compared to about 1.6 million tons of domestic production. In other words, PL 480 imports averaged about 14 per cent of domestic production. In addition, the superior quality of imported (hard) wheat under PL 480 and its comparatively lower price have positively influenced Greece's economy. This influence, however, was in a way indirect, for PL 480 wheat imports had less effect on the decisions of wheat producers than it had on government policy, which was to support prices, thereby increasing budget deficits. In particular, the government's policy of setting high support prices for wheat and fixed prices for bread could not have been maintained without wheat imports at low prices, such as those made possible under PL 480 programs, especially in the first years of the program. Further, during certain years the deficit of domestic production was so large that without PL 480 programs the government would have had either to import wheat through free-trade channels, and thus use up foreign exchange reserves, or to follow a much stronger protectionist system for wheat, aiming at providing further incentives to farmers for shifting production out of other crops into wheat. Both these alternatives, however, would have been detrimental, for either of them would have led to undesirable changes in the money and commodities market, as well as in the price mechanism, thus affecting not only agriculture, but the entire export and import sectors.

In short, PL 480 wheat imports have contributed to economic development, even though indirectly, through their effect on quality and their making possible the government's high support price system, which in later years (1958-62) encouraged expansion of wheat production approaching the level of domestic consumption requirements. PL 480 wheat imports were continued throughout 1958-62, at a rate of about 100,000 tons per year, despite the increase in domestic production and even though local wheat was exported. (In 1959, 150,000 tons were exported.) This can be explained only by inventory fluctuations and the uncertainties about the size of crops, as well as by the fact that the wheat imported under Title I could not be substituted for domestic wheat, but was used for special baking purposes. Nevertheless, these imports of wheat even under conditions of local overproduction have been favorable, for they played an important role in putting support prices at high levels, thus further stimulating domestic production without proportionately adverse fiscal effects.

In addition to wheat imports, a considerable portion of PL 480 imports comprised livestock feeds, which have been in great domestic demand in Greece because both of existing inadequate production and increasing requirements for feeding the growing livestock population that has resulted from the government's efforts since 1957-58.

The livestock population in Greece is mainly composed of small, nomadic animals with relatively low yields. During recent years, the government embarked on a serious effort to improve both the composition and yields of the livestock population in Greece. This program, however, required a steady flow of livestock fodder and at appropriate prices. Toward this purpose, the PL 480 livestock feeds contributed considerably over the 1955-62 period.

Over this period, Greece produced quite inadequate

quantities of maize, barley, oats, etc., most of which were consumed by peasant farms; only a limited amount reached the market. This situation led to high prices as well as to uncertainty as regard to a steady flow in the supply of livestock. PL 480 livestock imports, which amounted to $35.6 million over the period under review, have contributed substantially to the development of a greater volume and a better variety of livestock products. Given the foreign exchange limitations of Greece, imports of livestock feeds without the PL 480 program would not have been realized. In addition, "in the event that importations of livestock fodder would have been permitted through the free trade, it is very doubtful if the same rational use of these imports, such as took place under the state program, would have been achieved in view of the insufficient demand."[34] PL 480 imports led to a better reserve-stock policy for livestock fodder in Greece, brought about a reduction in the storage costs of producers by freeing them of the need for maintaining disproportionately large reserves, and helped stabilize market prices at reasonable levels. All these developments, of course, have had their positive effects on agricultural productivity and on farm incomes as well.

Finally, PL 480 imports of seed oils amounted to about 74 thousand tons over the period under review, the purpose of these being to supplement stocks during poor crop years and to maintain prices at reasonable levels for consumers. The mixing of seed oil with olive oil has had some effect in lowering consumer prices both of mixed and pure oil, and this in turn has increased the export of olive oil.

The impact of PL 480 upon the productivity of the Greek economy has also been registered through the availability of sales proceeds to industrial and other enterprises under the provisions of the Cooley Amendment (104e). Cooley loans amounted to about 199 million drachmas, or $6.6 million, over the period under review, representing 6.2 per cent of total drachma deposits generated by the application of the Title I over the period 1955–62. This, of course, is too small an

---

34. Coutsoumaris, Westebbe, and Psilos, *op. cit.*, p. IV–46.

amount—compared with the total domestic net capital formation —to have exercised any important influence on industrial productivity. Nevertheless, for the enterprises concerned these loans have been considered very important, for they were used to finance expansion of productive facilities at lower than domestic market interest rates and over much longer periods of maturity. (Most loans were charged with 6 per cent interest rate, while the prevailing effective loan rates on the market ran well above 13-14 per cent annually.)

The PL 480, Title I program has also to be considered from the standpoint of its monetary and fiscal effects. In the earlier years, when monetary stability was beginning to be achieved and the government deficit was being reduced, this program made an important contribution in restraining inflation. The deflationary effect has been estimated at 306 million drachmas in 1955 and 650 million drachmas in 1956, during which years the price change was 7 and 8 per cent respectively, and the current budget deficit was 655 million and 490 million drachmas. In subsequent years, when price changes were very small and the current budget deficit changed into surplus, the deflationary effect of the PL 480 program was still important, ranging from 346 million drachmas in 1961 to 494 million in 1962.[35]

The Effects of Foreign Aid on Public Finance. Due to the low tax capacity of Greece and to the uneven income distribution and high rate of tax evasion, the possibilities of deriving adequate revenues for budget financing in Greece were very small. Thus, foreign aid was almost exclusively used to finance current budget deficits up to 1955 and 1956. Along with economic expenditures, foreign aid was also financing large military expenses throughout the postwar period. It was only after 1955 that foreign sources were partially replaced by domestic sources. This substitution was the result not only of the increased volume of domestic savings and rising per capita in-

---

35. *Ibid.*, p. VII-37.

comes, but also of the shift that took place in United States aid policy after 1953-54.[36]

Apart from the contribution of United States aid to financing current budget deficits, the public investment budget also absorbed considerable amounts of aid funds. Up to the fiscal year 1952-53, 8,654 million drachmas in foreign funds were absorbed by public investments that amounted to 9,247 million drachmas. After 1954-55, domestic sources as well as foreign loans were substantially used to finance public investments. Thus, government bonds and treasury bills, amounting to more than 7,500 million drachmas over the period 1954-63, and all surpluses obtained from the current budget, were used to finance government investment. In addition, public loans of more than 3,000 million drachmas were obtained from Germany, AID and the European Consortium after 1954, for the same purpose.

In short, foreign aid contributed largely to financing both the current budget and public investment deficits up to the mid-1950's, while in the subsequent period the reduced volume of aid funds only marginally contributed to public investment. Since 1966, the Greek government has put more emphasis on foreign direct private investment, as well as on financing specific public and private projects, mainly in tourist, agricultural, and manufacturing sectors. Toward this aim, the government has been negotiating with Litton Industries and other American and European private concerns for the preparation of feasibility reports upon which the projects will be subsequently financed through foreign capital, either by direct participation or loan funds, or by a combination of the two.

The Role of Government

The rate of growth in the 1948-65 period was also due to governmental policies designed to achieve a level of demand

---

36. For a more detailed analysis of United States aid policy to Greece, see Psilos, and Westebbe, *op. cit.*, pp. 98-101.

adequate for attaining the highest possible employment rate, domestic and international equilibrium, and maintaining or increasing the standard of living.

Public Spending

The actions of the government in securing a high level of effective demand are reflected in the level and composition of public spending. Up to 1956, the spending policy of the Greek government was shaped by the heavy budget deficits, which were inconsistent with the aim of economic development. Although monetary measures, to a certain extent, could control the inflationary expansion resulting from other sources, they were basically unable to prevent inflationary pressures generated by budgetary deficits. Hence, the annual spending programs of the government had to be conservative in nature, and the structure of spending favored the less inflationary outlays.

The ordinary budget deficit dropped from 1,313 million drachmas in 1950-51 to 161 million drachmas in 1952-53, rising again to 459 million drachmas in 1955-56. Public investment expenditure, on the other hand, was reduced from 2,439 million drachmas in 1950-51 to 1,275 million in 1953-54 and to 1,792 million in 1955-56, a considerably lower level than that of 1950-51. The resulting annual fiscal deficits were almost entirely covered by United States counterpart funds, generated from economic assistance programs over the 1950-56 period. Since 1957 the current budget regularly has showed a surplus, which up to 1963 averaged about 916 million drachmas annually, the total for the 1962-65 period being about 3,390 million drachmas. These surpluses contributed greatly to the financing of public investment, which increased at an annual rate of 21.4 per cent over the 1957-62 period and 5.9 per cent during 1962-65, as contrasted with the declining rate that we have noted during the 1950-56 period.

Up to 1961, public savings accounted for well over 50 per cent of the financing of government investment. However, since then this share has been dropping. It was 49.2 per cent in 1962, 47.5 per cent in 1963, 42.2 per cent in 1964, and 14.2 per cent in

1965. This substantial decline in the share contributed by public savings to the financing of government investment during recent years, has been offset by the rising participation of the banking system through the means of treasury bills, issued specifically to finance public investment projects, and through other credits to the central government, as well as by the increased participation of the domestic bond market. On the average, public savings financed 37.2 per cent of government fixed investment during the 1962-65 period; the capital market, 14.2 per cent; the banking system's credits and treasury bills, 38.4 per cent; and capital transfers, 10.2 per cent.

As already noted, the government's expenditure policy pursued over the 1948-65 period has been designed to influence the economy's effective demand in the direction of more productive activities and to maintain monetary stability. As a result, there has been a relative decline in current expenditures since 1948 as a per cent of GNP. Measured in current prices, government spending was 13 per cent of GNP in 1948-53; 12.1 per cent in 1954-57; 9.7 in 1958-60. It rose slightly to 10.6 in the 1961-64 period and to 11.3 per cent in 1965.

From the point of view of development, however, the composition of public expenditures is perhaps more significant than the level of the expenditure. Up to 1957, about half of current expenditures went for national defense purposes, while the share of education was less than 7 per cent in most years and the share of public administration ranged between 15 and 20 per cent. By contrast, current expenditures since 1958 has favored those activities which were expected to exercise a positive influence on the rate of economic growth. On the average, during the 1958-64 period; education absorbed 12.2 per cent of total current expenditures; public administration, 25.1 per cent; national defense, 38.5 per cent; health and social welfare, 7.0 per cent; justice, 5.4 per cent; and all other activities, 11.8 per cent.

Notwithstanding this large-scale government spending, however, the results have been disappointing in terms of increased economic growth. In the first place, national defense expenditures have continued to be excessive in recent years.

Even in the latter part of the 1950's, when internal political stability was well established and no external threats to Greece were present, national defense expenditure absorbed more than 6.5 per cent of GNP, a ratio considerably higher than that of other NATO countries with the exception of the United States. Second, expenditures on education, which are generally considered as improving the long-run growth potential of any economy, were quite inadequate throughout the period under review. Up to 1962, education was constantly absorbing less than 1 per cent of GNP, finally reaching the level of 1.2 per cent in 1963 and 1.4 per cent in 1964. Third, public expenditure policy was unfavorably influenced by the organizational bottlenecks existing in the public sector, expecially in public administration and public institutions. These public entities and institutions, operating in a bureaucratic manner, functioned as an important *restraint* on government policy.

Finally, the over-all spending policy of the Greek government was unfavorably influenced by its transfer payments policies throughout the period under review. On the one hand, over 80 per cent of the annual transfer payments granted by the government represented transfers to the agricultural population, aiming at protecting farm incomes through price support policies, and stimulating changes in the composition of crops in agriculture. These transfer payments programs were always the most inflationary threats to the Greek economy, and as such, they seem to have had little, if any, positive effect on the rate of growth. On the other hand, the large subsidies extended constantly to cover the deficits incurred by the state railways and other public entities, have had rather strong adverse effects on the economy. The continuous efforts of the Bank of Greece to cut these subsidies to the minimum and to readjust them so that they could contribute positively to the growth of the economy, may well support our argument that these subsidies programs only marginally affected the average rate of growth.[37] It should be mentioned in this respect that the *Five-year Development Plan,* 1966–70, prepared by the

---

37. X. Zolotas, *op. cit.*, pp. 114-116.

Center of Planning and Economic Research in 1965, proposed an entirely new subsidy program, with a relatively low rate of increase in subsidies—2.3 per cent annually—as compared with the 10.2 per cent annual increase during 1958-65.

Government Policies Affecting Private Demand

Throughout the postwar period, total private expenditures have been influenced by a series of fiscal and monetary measures adopted by the central government. Fiscal policy has affected private flows of funds, both through the structure and rates of taxation, while monetary policy has worked mainly through its impact upon the availability and cost of credits.

Fiscal Policy. Taxation policy in Greece has always been designed to facilitate the mobilization of domestic savings—both public and private—and to allocate capital in a satisfactory manner for promoting growth. Another basic consideration underlying tax policy has been the redistribution of personal incomes in Greece so as to minimize income inequalities and raise the saving capacity of the economy.

Tax policy up to 1955-56 was dominated by the need to raise sufficient revenues to reduce the persistent deficit in the current budget. But after 1957, tax policy was designed to promote various desirable kinds of investment and a better allocation of resources, coupled with the surplus budget and monetary stability established after 1956, this greatly contributed to economic growth.

Consistent with the objectives of the fiscal policy of the 1950-55 period, the government took measures to improve tax assessment and collection procedures. Although these measures led to substantial increases in tax revenue over these years, they also resulted in a greater inequality of personal income because they favored the upper-income groups and led to a higher cost of production in certain sectors.[38]

However, despite these adverse effects, it should be pointed out that quite a few tax laws passed over the 1950-55 period

---

38. X. Zolotas, *op. cit.*, p. 107.

made a positive contribution to economic growth, although this cannot be quantified so as to demonstrate the net effects of tax policy on the rate of economic growth.

The first important tax law, passed in 1951, substituted a progressive tax rate (15 to 35 per cent) in place of the proportional rate (36 per cent) previously in effect on income from buildings, land, and securities. At the same time, the tax rates on profits earned by industrial firms were reduced.

Another growth-stimulating tax law, passed in 1953, protected foreign private capital in Greece. This law extended special tax benefits over a period of 10 years to export and mining enterprises, to repatriated Greek-owned ships, and to any other enterprises saving substantial amounts of foreign exchange. The law provided that the amount of income tax can be fixed at current rates for a 10-year period, or taxes can be levied at a fixed percentage of net or gross earnings at a rate lower than the current tax rate. The law also granted a number of other tax benefits, including concessions on the customs duties on imported machinery.

The tax legislation of 1954 established supplementary depreciation rates of up to 2.5 per cent on buildings constructed since 1947 and up to 6 per cent on other fixed assets acquired after that year. Further, the normal and supplementary depreciation rates applicable to manufacturing, mining, and hotel enterprises located outside the District of Attica were increased 100 per cent; if these enterprises were located within Attica, but outside Athens, the rates were increased 50 per cent.

Since the mid-1950's the major reforms in Greece have been the introduction of the new unified, progressive income tax in 1956 and the extension of the personal unified income tax to corporations, with taxation of undistributed profits at a rate of 35 per cent. In addition, to encourage productive investment the depreciation rates were raised and tax incentives were introduced. In 1956-57, all private loans and preferred stocks issued exclusively for the purpose of development investment were exempted from income tax and other charges. Income on deposits and on bonds issued by private and government utilities were also exempted. Further, other laws provided tax incentives on net profits and merging or expanding firms, while measures related to collection of taxes were taken. In 1958, the whole structure of indirect taxes was reformed so as to reduce consumption expenditures on luxury goods.

In general, the structure of tax revenues over the period 1958-65 did not change significantly, in spite of the new tax legislation over these years. The ratio of direct taxes to GNP ranged between 6.5 and 7.3 per cent, and averaged 6.8 per cent over the entire period, while indirect taxes ranged between 9.9 and 11.7 per cent and averaged 10.6 per cent. This tax revenue pattern is explained by the low per capita income of Greece, as well as by the high degree of tax evasion, due partly to the tax-evasion mentality of Greeks and partly to the complex and inefficient tax collection system. Notwithstanding these inefficiencies in the Greek tax system, however, the new indirect taxes and the tax concessions granted over the years under review have contributed to higher rates of investment in the private sector. Furthermore, monetary stability was substantially assisted by these tax measures, both in the short-run as well as in the long-run. As far as their effect on the formation of savings is concerned, one cannot reach a definite conclusion. We can only say that these policies led to a redistribution of financial savings in Greece, which had a positive influence upon the rate of growth, as described in the following section.

Monetary Policy

Monetary policy everywhere is principally a short-term instrument manipulated by the government according to the prevailing cyclical and even seasonal economic conditions. Hence, a detailed analysis of monetary policy in Greece lies outside the scope of this study. What follows is a description of the main monetary measures that in the opinion of the writer have had long-lasting effects on Greece's economic growth.

The responsibility for controlling money supply and credit was vested in the so-called Currency Committee, established in 1946 in accordance with an agreement between the British and Greek governments concerning the economic assistance to be given to Greece by Great Britain. At the time of its formation, the Currency Committee consisted of the Minister of Finance; the Minister of Coordination; the Governor of the Bank of Greece; and two foreign experts, representing Britain and the United States, who were vested with a veto on all actions.

Up to 1951, the guiding principle of monetary policy seems to have been the achievement of monetary stability at all costs. The Currency Committee, upon insistence of the United States representative, decided to restrict substantially all expansionary expenditures, including those funds available for reconstruction, by "blocking" large amounts of counterpart funds. The main argument was that if excessive American aid funds were made available to the Greek government, there would be inflationary pressures due to bottlenecks and inelasticity in production, as well as to the high level of military expenditure required by the Civil War and by Greece's North Atlantic Treaty Organization (NATO) obligations thereafter. Throughout the period 1948-52, the Greek government was forced by the American Mission to follow a fiscal and monetary policy aimed at keeping the aggregate demand at low levels. This restrictive expenditure policy was abandoned only after important changes took place both in the economic and political scene in the period 1952-54.

The return to more normal economic and political conditions after 1955 made it possible for monetary policy to be used more effectively, particularly as the volume of domestic saving increased and the banking system based its lending activities more upon its own funds than on Central Bank's finances.[39] Further, the new institutional reforms introduced in 1954,[40] as well as the relative revival of the securities market after 1957 and the appearance of budget surpluses thereafter, contributed

---

39. Indeed, up to 1954-55 all commercial banks in Greece had to rely upon central bank lending, because bank deposits virtually melted away during the postwar period. About 70 or 80 per cent of total bank loans were made possible by the Bank of Greece up to 1954, whereas this percentage was substantially reduced, falling from 70 per cent in 1952 to 50 per cent in 1954 and to 31.0 per cent in 1965.
40. See p. 66.

to the efficacy of monetary policy. Throughout the period of 1953-65, monetary policy, relatively speaking, was expansionary. As was observed in the section on *The Growth Record*, the stock of money increased much faster than GNP at current prices, and in some years the large differential increases in these two variables reflected short-term monetary policy actions of the government. To summarize, the principal forces responsible for such large fluctuations in the supply of money beyond the increases in GNP have been: deficit financing of the agricultural sector, heavy defense expenditures, and the government's effort to utilize fully the development potential of the economy. All these factors meant that the monetary authority had not much choice but to follow an *easy* money policy over the period under review. Fortunately, however, this was accompained by a rise in domestic manufacturing production, which in association with devaluation and with increasing exports (financed by the rapidly accumulating foreign exchange receipts from exports and invisible sources) led to the restoration of monetary stability after 1956. And as has been indicated earlier, monetary stability, together with the recovery of the general public from the psychology of inflation, led to a rapid accumulation of deposits with financial institutions after 1956. As a result, time and savings deposits held by the public rose from 4,421 million drachmas in 1956 to 33,941 million drachmas at the end of 1965.

This rapid accumulation of liquid assets was partly facilitated, however, by the interest-rate policy on deposits, adopted by the Currency Committee, at least in the earlier years. Thus, the nominal interest rates on time and savings deposits were raised from 7 to 10 per cent in May 1956. The rate on savings deposits was reduced to 9 per cent in July 1957 for savings deposits and in January 1958 for time deposits. The rate on time deposits remained at 9 per cent up to September 1959, when it was reduced to 8 per cent, to be reduced again to 7 and 5.5 per cent in September 1959 and March 1960 respectively. Since then the average interest rates on time deposits of various maturities has ranged from 5.25 to 6.5 per cent. On the other hand, savings deposits which have a high degree of liquidity, since they are withdrawable at any time, earned 8.0 per cent over the period from January 1958 to May 1958, 7.5 per cent from May 1958 to January 1959, and 6.5 per cent from September 1959 to March 1960; since November 1960, they have earned 4.5 per cent on savings deposits with Commercial Banks, 4.75 per cent with the Agricultural Bank, and 5 per cent on savings deposits with the Postal Savings Bank.

In spite of this constant reduction of interest rates on deposits, however, savings and time deposits increased tremendously over the same period, both in absolute amounts and in terms of the number of deposit accounts. The latter increased from 168,520 at the end of 1955 to 1,394,000 at the end of 1963.[41]

The increase in the liquidity of the monetary system after 1958–59 led to a reduction of the cost of capital in Greece. Thus, bank rates on long-term industrial loans declined from 10 per cent in March 1957, to 9 per cent in July 1959, and to 7 per cent in October of the same year. The rediscount rate was accordingly reduced from 11 per cent in March 1957, to 10 per cent in April 1959, to 9 per cent in October 1959, to 7 per cent in April 1960, to 6 per cent in November of the same year, and to 5.5 per cent in April 1963. Comparable interest-rate reductions were made in all other categories of loans over the same period.

The reduction in the cost of capital, together with the more selective credit policies effected since 1956, has influenced greatly the economic expansion of various enterprises in Greece. The main emphasis of credit policy has been on the contribution of the particular enterprise or particular sector to the economic development of the country. The distribution of banking funds among competing sectors was influenced by selective credit controls. The basic weaknesses in the general quantitative controls and the inadequate mechanism of open-market operations, led the monetary authorities to rely chiefly on *special* quantitative and selective monetary instruments. These monetary regulations were continuously adjusted to whatever new developments were appearing in the economy. The following measures were taken over the 1954–65 period.

---

41. X. Zolotas, *op. cit.*, p. 67. No statistics are available for the period 1964–65.

(a) *Reserve Requirements.* Up to 1956, reserve requirements were set at the level of 12 per cent of bank deposits, including demand deposits. This ratio was reduced to 8 per cent in 1956 and to 5 per cent in October 1963, at which time the banks were given the option to invest 3 per cent of their demand and savings deposits in interest-bearing treasury bills. In 1957, the Currency Committee made it compulsory for banks to invest 10 per cent of these deposits in treasury bills; this reserve requirement was raised to 18 per cent in 1959 and to 20 per cent in 1963. Bankers expressed resentment of this measure, but the need of the central government to finance its investment program made repeal impossible. Over the 1957-65 period, commercial banks financed about 6.5 billion drachmas of government expenditures through their purchase of treasury bills. Hence, the compulsory investment in treasury bills played a significant role in controlling the availability of credit by reducing liquidity.

(b) *Discount Policy.* A discount policy was introduced in Greece in May 1956, when the Currency Committee began to allow the banks to rediscount industrial bills. The initial rate was 11 per cent, but this has fluctuated downward in subsequent years in order to counteract temporary shortages of funds in the banking system. This monetary instrument has functioned quite effectively since its first application in 1956, thus contributing to the flexible finance of the economy.

(c) *Managing Deposits of Public Entities.* The availability of bank credit was also influenced by the control-mechanism of deposits belonging to public entities and savings banks. From 1950 onward these funds, deposited with the commercial banks, were directly handled by the Currency Committee with the aim of promoting the export and industrial sectors of the economy. It is worth noting that funds made available to commercial banks in this way, increased from 857 million drachmas in 1958 to 1,252 million in 1965. Hence, the liquidity of commercial banks was augmented by these amounts.

(d) *Selective Credit Controls.* Selective controls in the credit sector were specifically designed to influence the use of bank funds to stimulate economic development. Credit ceilings and fixed rates of increase on loans were granted to various sectors of the economy to prevent structural imbalances in the price mechanism, as well as to wipe out sectoral shortages of funds. Up to 1957, such preventive controls were used in a variety of forms; in that year, banks were made responsible for whatever credit was extended to firms, on the assumption that the financial institutions were in a better position to control the borrowing enterprises. However, the large increase in industrial credits over the years 1957 and 1958, from 5.3 billion drachmas, by the end of 1956 to 8.6 billion drachmas by the end of 1958, proved that these institutions were not successfully distributing available funds and were unable to prevent the extensive leakage of credit to real estate and consumption sectors. In subsequent years, new rules were introduced by the Currency Committee affecting bank loans to manufacturing and other activities. The volume and distribution of credits granted to the private sector by the monetary system over the 1955–65 period is shown in Table 14.

Table 14: Credit Outstanding by Sectors (millions of drachmas)

Year	Agriculture Amount	% of Total	Manufacturing Amount	% of Total	Trade Amount	% of Total	Other Amount	% of Total
1955	3,749	33.2	4,358	38.7	1,693	15.0	1,475	13.0
1956	4,495	32.0	5,326	37.9	2,690	19.2	1,529	10.9
1957	5,602	31.6	7,128	40.2	3,307	18.6	1,711	9.6
1958	6,557	30.9	8,614	40.6	3,617	17.1	2,408	11.4
1959	7,637	32.6	9,209	39.3	3,847	16.4	2,752	11.7
1960	8,194	30.0	10,911	39.9	4,283	15.7	3,960	14.5
1961	9,272	30.0	12,146	39.4	4,482	14.5	4,947	16.0
1962	10,086	28.0	14,006	38.8	6,136	17.0	5,821	16.2
1963	10,916	25.2	16,704	38.6	7,689	17.8	8,003	18.5
1964	13,092	26.2	19,132	38.3	8,381	16.8	9,355	18.7
1965	16,204	28.9	20,765	37.1	8,717	15.6	10,344	18.5

Source: *Monthly Bulletin* of the Bank of Greece.

In all, only a small portion of the economy has been influenced by the volume of bank credits since 1955, as is indicated by the low ratio, as compared with gross national product, of new loans granted by the entire monetary system; this ratio has ranged from 1.6 to 3.7 per cent of GNP. The index of total credits in the economy to total liabilities declined steadily from 100 in 1955 to 37.1 in 1965. The decline in this index points to an important conclusion with respect to the monetary and financial developments in Greece: the banking system has had *excess liquidity* over the entire period, 1955-65.

*Policies Affecting the
Allocation of Resources*

The rate of growth of the Greek economy has also been influenced by certain government measures specifically designed to improve the resource allocation mechanism. Institutional changes, as well as specific regional incentives, were introduced in a variety of forms during the entire postwar period. A first step toward this was the reformation of the Greek administration undertaken at the termination of the Civil War in September 1949. A better coordinating mechanism, which tended to reduce substantially bureaucratic confusion and procedural overlapping, was created by the reorganization of the Ministry of Coordination and by the formation, during the early reconstruction period, of the following main agencies: the Marshall Plan Committee in 1947; the Supreme Council for Reconstruction in May 1948; the Division for Coordination and Application of Reconstruction Programs in August 1948, and the Central Loan Committee in November 1948.

Throughout the postwar period a number of foreign specialists assisted in this effort to improve the government administration apparatus. In 1947, the Foreign Trade Administration was established, by agreement between the American and Greek governments, for the purpose of administering and coordinating foreign trade policies. Moreover, foreign specialists helped in setting up, in the Ministry of Coordination, the National Statistical Service and the Division of National Accounts, both of which have provided extremely valuable help to the planners of economic policy. Furthermore, a 1953 decree established the Greek Productivity Center for the purpose of disseminating information about modern methods of production. The application of scientific research and the education of business leaders, by means of seminars, lectures, and other programs, have been the main instruments used by the Productivity Center. Closely cooperating with specialists of OECD, the Productivity Center has concluded many studies concerning scientific research and methodology.

The regional allocation of available national resources was considerably improved by the large investment expenditure on social overhead projects. Transportation, communication, electricity, and construction increased their share of gross investment from 57.8 per cent in 1948–52 to 65.4 per cent in 1953–57, though this declined to 63.3 per cent in 1958–61. By comparison, manufacturing's share was 32.9 per cent, 22.7 per cent, and 28.3 per cent respectively during those same periods.

In the field of electric power, Greek regional economic development was facilitated after 1954 by hydroelectric plants installed in four key regions of the country: (a) the Ladon Hydroelectric Plant, in the Central Peloponnese, with two units of a total installed capacity of 70,000 KW, commenced operating on February 1, 1955; (b) the Agra Hydroelectric Plant, near Edessa in Central Macedonia, with two units of total installed capacity of 50,000 KW, commenced operating in July 1954; (c) the Louros Hydroelectric Plant, In Epirus, with two units of a total installed capacity of 5,000 KW, commenced operating on March 20, 1954; and (d) the Tavropos Hydroelectric Plant (Megdova), in Central Thessaly, with three units of a total installed capacity of 120,000 KW, commenced operating in November 1960, February 1961, and August 1962 respectively. Further, in 1961 the Public Power Corporation (PPC) bought out the Athens-Piraeus Power Company and thus added to its existing capacity an additional 198,750 KW. By this expanding and integrating of a multitude of power producing units, the PPC was able to make the most efficient use of the power generated throughout Greece and to eliminate inefficient units in many areas. To this expanded production, must be added the extensive transmission network of PPC, with an operating voltage of 150,000 v. Thus, by December 1963, a total of 5,384,000 inhabitants were serviced by PPC, 62 per cent of whom were outside the Athens-Piraeus area.

In the field of finance, two important institutional changes in 1954 significantly facilitated the allocation of productive services in Greece. A Public Development Bank (Economic Development Financing Organization [EDFO]) was established to accomplish two missions: first, to collect $78.5 million in frozen credits granted between 1948 and mid-1954 by the American Mission for Aid to Greece and by its successor, the Central Loan Committee; second, to grant medium- and long-term loans to industrial, mining, tourist, and agricultural enterprises and to participate in these enterprises through preferred stock. Generally speaking, this organization was successful in handling these loans, although its performance left much to be desired. Compared, however, with the operations of the Central Loan Committee, which allocated funds in fields that lacked entrepreneurial and managerial efficiency, optimum economic size, and modern techniques and method of production, EDFO has indeed shown a much better record of performance.

The second institutional reform in 1954 was the merging of two commercial banks (the National Bank and the Bank of Athens) into one National Bank, strongly influenced by the government. Although this merger reduced competition in the banking business, it also led to greater efficiency in the financial system at that time and greater public confidence in the banking business. The immediate result was a rapid accumulation of deposits with the financial institutions and a lower cost of capital resulting in part from economies of scale.

These institutional reforms, together with the selective and general monetary measures applied by the Currency Committee for the past decade, have contributed to a better allocation of available funds. Since 1957, commercial banks have been allowed to grant long-term loans to industrial firms, whereas up to that time they could only grant short-term credit, which was renewed and played the role of revolving credit. By 1963, the amount of new long-term credit was about five times greater than in 1954, while long-term debt as a percentage of over-all debt averaged 31.1 per cent over the same period.

Hence, capital formation in the more productive sectors of the economy was subjected to the test of the capital market, as compared to the large dependence of Greek firms on short-term (revolving) bank credit, which had made them very sensitive to conditions of "increasing risk" and therefore had fostered conservative policies. Indeed, the larger proportion of short-term bank credits up to 1957-58 had imposed—on small firms in particular—onerous interest rates, hiked by commission and service charges. Small firms therefore tended to reinvest whatever profits were earned and to refrain from borrowing or resorting to capital-market financing, which limited growth to the availability of profits. The rational credit policy applied after 1957 has played an important role in accustoming businessmen to conditions of "increasing risk" and to adopt less conservative policies. Likewise, it has forced lenders to charge substantially less than before on long-term borrowed capital.

As this suggests, government policy in different periods has had varying effects on the competitive climate in Greece. In the earlier postwar years, the government's policy—not only as regards bank credit but in other vital areas as well—tended to encourage a conservative, protectionist attitude among Greek businessmen.

Direct governmental intervention in the private sector has been partly responsible for the stifling of competition. The chief vehicle for this intervention has been the "certificate of expediency" required for establishing, locating, expanding or merging businesses. Thus, entry has often been blocked by the refusal of the Ministry of Industry, to grant "expediency licenses" for the establishment of new factories or for the expansion of existing ones. The consequence has been a high-cost industrial structure, large sectors of which are under monopoly control, with little incentive to undertake innovations or to use capital in an optimum manner. "Protection may have raised the marginal efficiency of capital in industries producing goods complementary to the protected industries."[42] Furthermore, government tariff policy, at least up to 1953, was strongly pro-

---

42. Ellis, Psilos, and Westebbe, *op. cit.*, p. 267.

tectionist, while a system of licensing, based on import quotas designed to preserve scarce foreign exchange, was combined with the tariff structure. This perpetuated a large number of small firms dedicated to the preservation of inefficient methods and sheltered position.

In recent years, however, broad shifts in government economic policy have helped to change this picture and to create a more competitive climate. We have noted the changes in the tax structure that were designed to promote development through the encouragement both of larger industrial units and of the geographic decentralization of industry. The system of "expediency permits" was also changed to further these objectives. Moreover, the government's policy to reduce inefficiency and waste in the use of resources—as in the case of the electric power industry—has been quite effective. Better coordination of finance and regional planning at the local government level likewise has contributed to a better utilization of public financial resources, resulting in an improved allocation of real resources in the economy as a whole.

Finally, the liberalization of imports after 1954 also played a vital role in improving the allocation of factors of production. As a result of the liberalization of foreign trade, imports rose from 6,904 million drachmas in 1953, to 9,703 million in 1954, and to a record 15,756 million in 1958, an increase which cannot be entirely explained by economic variables. This liberal import policy was thought to be a positive contribution to economic development; accordingly, the monetary and fiscal policies of the government were designed to influence all the components of the balance of payments, though focused primarily on the pattern of imports, exports, and invisibles. Import quotas were removed to an extent matched at that time by only a few European countries.[43] New taxation and foreign exchange policies were established for the protection of Greek-owned ships transferred from flags of convenience to the Greek flag. Tax incentives and other institutional facilities were provided for foreign capital. All these measures led to significant in-

---

43. X. Zolotas, *op. cit.*, p. 128.

creases in foreign exchange earnings from invisible sources, which rose from $74.4 million in 1952, to $124.2 million in 1954, to $235.7 million in 1957, and to $481 million in 1966. At the risk of repetition, the most important components of these invisible receipts have been emigrants' remittances which financed 48 per cent of trade deficit over the period 1957–63 and 32 per cent in 1963–66, as compared with 42 per cent of shipping and tourist's receipts over the period 1957–63 and 43 per cent in 1963–66.

In short, the institutional reforms introduced after 1953 and the *liberalization* of imports, together with export incentives and other direct and indirect government measures that followed, undoubtedly led to a higher degree of competition in the domestic market. To all these measures should be added the considerable technical assistance received from the OECD and other European economic, technical, and research organizations throughout the 1954–64 period, as well as the growing awareness among Greek entrepreneurs of increasing competition from Common Market industries. This potential competition has forced the Greek entrepreneurs—especially the large ones—to give thought to improving internal organizational efficiency and raising the standard of management and skills in general by hiring foreign specialists or foreign-trained Greeks.

Memoranda of Comment, Reservation, or Dissent

Pages 8 and 30—By CHARLES P. KINDLEBERGER, *Member, CED Research Advisory Board:*

In my judgment, Dr. Psilos pays rather too little attention to the role of emigration in Greek economic growth since the war and especially in the 1960's. On page 8, with a reference to the loss of labor skills, he calls emigration a mixed blessing. On page 30 there is reference to emigrant remittances, which covered half the trade deficit over the period 1957–63. Elsewhere he mentions the burden of unemployment and underemployment. I would contend, however, that in Greece, as well as in Southern Italy, Spain, and Portugal, emigration is a stimulus to growth not only through its contribution to foreign exchange, which uses up no domestic resources, and to savings, which are substantial, but because of its assistance in restoring price incentives.

When there is considerable unemployment and underemployment, the incentive to invest capital to replace labor is seriously weakened. The removal of excess labor raises the marginal productivity of labor to the wage rate and restores prices incentives in the capital market. This raises both investment and growth.

Dr. Psilos also pays little attention throughout his paper to education and improvements in the quality of the labor force. While emigration does occasion some loss in labor skills, the ultimate return of temporary migrants and successful Greek attempts to appeal to students abroad to return have been significant counterweights.

These points are made to call attention to what seem to me to be omissions in Dr. Psilos' otherwise admirable account.

Appendix

Notes on the Difficulties of Economic Planning in Greece

Throughout the postwar period, Greece has not had a well-defined and consistent growth policy in the sense of striving *consciously* for a given set of development targets. Only sporadic attempts were made to plan the allocation of resources.

The first such attempt was undertaken in 1948, out of which a four-year reconstruction plan emerged and was submitted to Organization for European Economic Corporation (OEEC) for approval. This planning procedure was required for all European countries that were receiving United States aid at the time.

The major objectives of this reconstruction plan were formulated in a very general framework, in which emphasis was given to rehabilitation of Greece's financial, monetary, and credit system; attainment of the highest possible rate of employment; development of natural resources; and achievement of equilibrium in Greek international accounts, by increasing exports and reducing imports.

In this plan, United States direct and indirect economic aid was supposed to play the most important role, and the aid requested amounted to $1,186 million. Of this, $573 million was to finance imports, mainly foodstuffs and other essentials, and the remaining $613 million was to cover domestic expenditures.[44]

In addition to this four-year plan, the Government Supreme Council of Reconstruction prepared a one-year program for 1948–49, which was also submitted to OEEC following approval by ECA. For this program, the Greek government requested $285 million in United States aid, but OEEC, with the approval of ECA, allocated $211.6 million, of which $144.8 million was in the form of net drawing rights.

Neither the 1948–52 four-year plan nor the 1948–49 program was successfully implemented. In the first place, the lack of government stability did not present the necessary continuity of action and responsibility for carrying out the planned allocation of resources. Secondly, inflationary pressures created distortions, and large sums were transferred from reconstruction to current accounts in order to prevent domestic price rises and offset budgetary deficits. In addition, procedural delays and institutional bottlenecks, as well as delays in the conclusion of

---

44. Bank of Greece, *Report of the Governor, 1948*, Athens, 1949, p. 18.

bilateral trade agreements made it difficult for the authorities to proceed according to plan.

True, planning in any but authoritarian economic systems is in a sense presumptuous; without control over all decision to be made by every economic unit, no plan can be fulfilled in detail. Yet, planning of some sort is necessary, otherwise *ad hoc* economic policy decisions made by individual policy makers can lead to serious inconsistencies and a wasting of the country's resources.

Such was, however, the situation in Greece throughout the 1950's. During this period no long-term economic planning was contemplated with a systematic and consistent framework of targets and policies. There were only *ad hoc* economic policies made by individual ministries or by Parliament with respect to specific projects and public works. It was only in 1959 that the government published for the first time a five-year plan; this grew out of the work of the Research Committee for the Organization of Economic Planning, which had been established by the government in 1957. This committee published a series of reports on the performance of various sectors and the need of these sectors for further development, and it then compiled and classified the statistical data that went into the five-year plan. The plan was quickly revised a year later (1960) to include objectives for a period of 10 years. The target for the annual rate of growth was 6 per cent, with 3.5 per cent annual increase for agricultural income, 8.1 per cent for industry, and 6.6 per cent for services. Total employment was to reach 4 million in 1969. The competitiveness of the Greek industry was to be encouraged in order to meet the stiff competition of the Common Market countries. Regional income and productivity disparities were to be minimized by 1969 through regional development. All these aims were translated into specific, detailed objectives for the first five years and more general objectives for the second five years.

However, the performance of the Greek economy over the 1960–64 period far exceeded the specific goals of the five-year plan, proving its poor and unscientific basis. For instance, the rate of growth of the economy, measured in terms of gross national income at 1954 prices, varied from 2.9 per cent in 1962 to 11 per cent in 1961, averaging 7.5 per cent per annum over the period 1959–64. Industrial output also exceeded the planned goals, the average annual increase having been 9.7 per cent as compared with the 8.1 per cent planned.

The crucial test of the plan is to be sought in the investment ratio, which according to the plan would rise from 16.3 per cent of GNP in 1959 to 23 per cent in 1964. Total investment in fixed assets, however, actually increased at a rate of only 12.0 per cent over the 1959–64 period, while private investment in manufacturing increased at a much lower rate. This has been due partly to uncertainties among businessmen with respect to the Common Market, partly to inconsistent government policies affecting the investment behavior of the private sector.

Likewise, it had been anticipated that the increase in imports would run about 8 per cent annually for the first five years of the plan, whereas imports actually rose annually at an average rate of 13 per cent. As regards exports, the expectation was an increase at an annual average rate of 8.1 per cent, but in fact exports declined by 4 per cent in 1960 and then increased by 12 per cent in 1961, 5 per cent in 1962, 22 per cent in 1963, and 1.4 per cent in 1964, the average annual increase being 7.2 per cent.

The public investment targets of the program showed a worse performance than private investment. Thus, 92 per cent of scheduled public investment was undertaken as compared with 94 per cent of scheduled private investment. Moreover, the capital formation that did occur in the public sector had less effect on economic growth than the planners had calculated. Public investment expenditures were not distributed among the various projects as anticipated in the plan. For instance, due to poor evaluation of particular public works, many productive—or relatively productive—projects were finally excluded from the program in order to finance other less productive undertakings, while the financial outlay on these projects reached levels two or three times higher than the original planned cost. In road construction, irrigation, and tourism, some projects surpassed their original estimated outlay by more than 300–400 per cent, amounting to hundreds of millions of drachmas each year. Of course, technical difficulties were undoubtedly involved, but political considerations and the lack of feasibility studies for the majority of public works should be held responsible for this misuse of capital.[45]

The problem of planning economic development in Greece recently has been approached for the first time in a scientific manner, by the Center of Planning and Economic Research (CPER).* Staffed with American-trained Greek and foreign economists, CPER was established in Athens late in 1964 and charged with the responsibility of preparing a five-year development program with various alternative growth targets, the final choice of which would rest with the government.

By the end of 1965, the Center submitted to the government a plan for the 1966–70 period with these main objectives:

An annual average rate of increase of gross domestic product at constant prices, on the order of 7–8 per cent over the 1966–70 period.

Average gross income per capita, at constant prices, to increase from $570 in 1965 to $800 in 1970.

An increase in the national product, arising mainly out of increases in productivity, whose over-all rate of growth is ex-

---

45. There are many well-known cases of such projects, but the most highly publicized one is the public fertilizer plant in the Ptolemais region. The feasibility study of this project, undertaken by foreign groups, led to the erection of the fertilizer factory in 1959. This factory has not as yet started producing normally. Its cost was originally estimated at $40 million but present calculations put it well above $65 million. Most of the excess cost was incurred in providing infrastructure, such as rail lines to the lignite mines and electric transmission equipment, the cost of which apparently had not been foreseen in the original study. More disturbing are reports that lignite deposits at the site are not sufficient to supply the fertilizer plant after the new electric power plant begins to operate by the end of this year. Thus, it will be necessary to transport fuel oil from Salonica for the operation of the plant, thus adding to the cost per unit of output. Furthermore, the water project, which is to supply water to the fertilizer plant through an artificial lake (Perthika Lake), has encountered serious difficulties. Recent reports indicate that the dam constructed on the river is useless: unexpected holes at its bottom prevent the lake from filling up in the summer, while in the winter it contains water only as a result of the natural flow from upstream. Another example of the misuse of capital is the famous Mont Parnes Hotel, which cost about 110 million drachmas, as compared with the original estimate of 15 million drachmas.

*Editor's Note: As Senior Economist of the Center, Dr. Psilos speaks with first-hand knowledge of the subject.

pected to be 6.4 per cent annually up to 1970. Productivity in manufacturing is expected to increase at a rate of 8.6 per cent; in agriculture, 6.2 per cent; in public utilities, 9.2 per cent; in construction, 4.2 per cent; and in other services, 3.7 per cent. The emphasis given to the rapid increase in productivity is explained, of course, by the need to adapt Greece's economy within a short time period to the conditions of the developed European economies that are members of the Common Market.

A particularly high increase in the rate and pattern of employment of high productivity activities. Likewise, it is expected that unemployment and underemployment will be reduced to normal levels and that net emigration will return to a low level.

A more equitable distribution of income, among income groups and geographical regions. As an example, real wages are planned to increase at 4.5 to 5.0 per cent annually over the 1966-70 period, which would close the gap between annual increases in output and real wages prevailing up to 1965. This gap has been estimated at 20 per cent for the period 1958-63.[46] A series of measures is proposed in one plan, the implementation of which would lead to high increases in agricultural incomes relative to the average growth, as well as to wage increases relative to the rest of the nonagricultural classes.

Regarding the distribution of financial resources during the 1966-70 period, domestic saving is estimated at 243.9 billion drachmas for the five-year period, covering about 90 per cent of total investment requirements. Of this amount, about 54.5 billion drachmas would represent public savings, the remainder private gross saving. The financial deficit for the economy as a whole is estimated at 27 billion drachmas for the period; this would be financed by foreign resources. The required gross inflow of resources from abroad, however, would have to be about 40 billion drachmas to ensure equilibrium in the balance of payments during the 1966-70 period.

Public expenditures, at constant 1965 prices, are estimated to increase from 19.8 billion drachmas in 1965 to 28,000 million

---

46. See *Draft of the Five Year Economic Development Plan for Greece, 1966-1970: A Summary* (Athens: Center of Planning and Economic Research, 1965), p. 14.

in 1970, rising at 7.2 per cent annually. Private consumption, on the other hand, would increase from 117.1 billion in 1965 to 161.6 billion drachmas in 1970, rising at 6.7 per cent annually. Gross investments, required to secure the 7-8 per cent annual growth of the economy, would rise from 39.3 billion drachmas in 1965 to 63.1 billion in 1970, increasing at 9.9 per cent annually. Of this amount, the private sector would be responsible for 34.2 billion drachmas in terms of gross fixed asset formation in 1970, rising at 5.3 per cent annually, and the public sector for 23.0 billion, increasing at 19.1 per cent.

With regard to the evolution of Greece's balance of payments, the five-year plan set forth the following objectives: (a) The foreign capital requirements, especially in terms of loan funds, were estimated to represent only 3.2 per cent of GNP in 1970 as compared to 5.0 per cent in 1965. (b) The foreign exchange reserves with the Bank of Greece were set to be kept throughout the plan period at 25 per cent of the value of goods to be imported annually. This relatively high percentage was mainly justified on the grounds that the main foreign exchange inflows, such as shipping remittances, emigrants, and tourist receipts, are vulnerable to changes in the international conditions. (c) The structure of exports during the period 1966-70 was planned to be improved. Thus, exports of manufactures were planned to rise from 21 per cent of total exports in 1965 to 30.8 per cent in 1970. Correspondingly, nonmanufacturing exports were planned to decline in relative terms. Of total agricultural exports, tobacco, raisins, and currants were estimated to drop from 62.5 per cent of total agricultural exports in 1965 to 48.5 per cent in 1970. (d) On the import side, the five-year plan estimated an annual rate of increase of total imports equal to 10.5 per cent, at constant 1961 prices, as against the 12 per cent which would result if past trends were to continue.

The above specific objectives of the five-year plan would be achieved mainly through effective changes in the over-all structure of Greece's economy, through changes on a wide scale of public institutions (including public administration) and through the application of special measures to wipe out the existing bottlenecks in some activities and enlarge the supply of labor and managerial skills, etc., all of which were expected to lead to higher productivity rates. It goes without saying, that the accomplishment of the above targets was expected to take place in an environment of a mixed economy, the state giving its fullest support to private initiative by eliminating or minimizing all unjustified restrictions to business enterprises. Among these restrictions, the minimization of bureaucratic practices, as well as the elimination of monopolistic restraints in the private sector are given high priority.

In short, the five-year plan prepared by CPER in late 1965 was a well-balanced document. Both its statistical forecasts and policy measures, were based on the theoretical and empirical background of a large number of internationally well-known Greek and foreign economists. But to our regret, however, the plan has never been implemented. It became instead a politically controversial issue immediately after it was submitted to the government. As a result, the plan was turned over early in 1966, for a critical review, to an *ad hoc* committee consisting of a number of academic, business, and government people. Almost a year later, this committee, chaired by Professor A. Agelopoulos, submitted to the Greek government another document, which in effect approved almost all the objectives and targets of the plan. The differences were largely matters of emphasis rather than policy. An important contribution of this committee was its special emphasis on the need of implementing the five-year plan as soon as possible. But despite this general agreement, nothing further has happened, and it is the belief of the people involved that the plan will remain purely an academic document, to the discouragement of the group of prominent economists who prepared it.

2.

The Characteristics of Israel's Economic Growth

Nadav Halevi

The Author

NADAV HALEVI is Senior Lecturer in economics at the Hebrew University of Jerusalem. Born in the United States, he graduated from the University of Cincinnati in 1950 and received his doctorate in economics at Columbia University in 1956. Mr. Halevi served as a research economist with the Falk Project Economic Research in Israel, then joined the Israel Ministry of Finance as economic advisor to the Foreign Exchange Division in 1957. Since 1960 he has taught at the Hebrew University. His publications include *Estimates of Israel's International Transactions: 1952–54* and *The Development of the Israel Economy*, as well as various monographs and articles on Israel's economy and international trade.

Contents

Introductory Note	83
The Pre-State Background	84
Immigration and Economic Growth	86
Economic Growth	88
Capital Inflow	98
World Jewry	101
United States Government	102
West Germany	102
Economic Policy	104
The Tools of Policy	104
The Shifts in Economic Policy	108
Problems and Prospects	113
Appendix: Summary of Positive and Negative Factors	115

Tables

1:	Population of Israel, 1948–65	87
2:	Growth of Gross National Product, 1950–65	89
3:	Industrial Origin of Net Domestic Products	90
4:	Civilian Labor Force and Unemployment, 1949–65	92
5:	Structure of Jewish Employment, Selected Years	94
6:	Resources at the Disposal of the Economy and Their Uses, 1950–66	96
7:	Real Resources and Their Uses, 1950–66	97
8:	Balance of Payments, 1949–65	99
9:	Main Sources of Long-Term Capital Inflow, 1949–65	100
10:	Money Supply and Cost-of-Living Index, 1948–66	110

Introductory Note

In the two decades that have elapsed since Israel achieved independence in 1948, economic development has proceeded at a tremendous pace. Israel's experience differs from that of other developing countries in two major respects: first, the population by and large is a transplanted population; second, Israel has received a massive capital inflow, resulting mainly from the conscious desire of Jews throughout the world to participate in the absorption of immigrants and the development of the country.

This brief survey concentrates on the main factors affecting growth. A short review of the pre-state background is followed by a discussion of the growth in population, since it is this that has created the need for very rapid development. Next, the magnitudes of economic growth and of the factors explaining it are analyzed. Finally, there is a discussion of the role of economic policy.[1]

Israel's growth of course has been affected by many factors other than those that have been stressed in this paper. To bring these many elements into perspective, the author has compiled a list of the factors that have affected economic growth either negatively or positively. This will be found in the Appendix.

---

1. This paper is based largely on a three-year study of the Israel economy by N. Halevi and R. Khnov-Malul for the List Institute Israel Project. This comprehensive study is being published under the title *The Economic Development of Israel* by the Bank of Israel and Frederick A. Praeger. Full references and acknowledgements will be found in that work, but special thanks for helpful comments on a previous draft of this paper are due to Y. Attiya, S. Freund, C. P. Kindleberger, and M. J. Sarnat.

The Pre-State Background

Though Jewish efforts to rebuild Palestine as a national homeland started in 1882, they gained great momentum with the occupation of Palestine by British forces in 1917 and the subsequent replacement of Ottoman rule by a League of Nations Mandate held by Britain, which specifically called for the development of a Jewish National Homeland. During the thirty years of the Mandate, Palestine was transformed from an undeveloped, underpopulated country into a rapidly developing modern economy. But the increase in the Jewish population, from one-tenth of the population of Palestine at the beginning of the period to one-third at its close, aroused Arab antagonism to the Mandate, although in absolute terms the Arab population had grown more. Arab hostility to the authorities erupted in 1929 and more seriously in 1936-39 because Jewish immigration was not curbed sufficiently to suit Arab demands, and when Arab demands were satisfied after World War II, the Jews became hostile. The British administration found itself in a dilemma, which it handed over to the United Nations. The UN decision to partition Palestine was rejected by the Arabs, whose armies were unable, however, to prevent the emergence of an independent state of Israel in May 1948.

The British viewed their task as the provision of law and order and of some of the prerequisites for economic development, but did not accept any active initiative in economic development. This policy was not unacceptable to the Jewish institutions (chief among them the Jewish Agency for Palestine), which were quite ready to accept the responsibility for initiating development. In fact, the development of Jewish Palestine was recognized by the Zionist Movement as the task of world Jewry. There were complaints, however, that the British administration hampered the work of development, particularly by curbing Jewish immigration.

During the Mandate period, about half a million Jewish immigrants came to Palestine, in several distinct waves of immigration. Most came in response to adverse conditions abroad; in fact, the flow to Israel was but part of a large stream of Jewish emigration from eastern and later central Europe. As world immigration restrictions mounted, particularly in the United States in the 1920's, more Jews turned to Palestine. Yet a substantial number of immigrants to Palestine were idealists, who wanted to build a new type of economic and social life in Palestine. They were instrumental in setting up new types of agricultural settlements and other economic and social undertakings which led to the development of the country.

These people, highly educated, idealistic, and dedicated as they were, would not have been enough to convert the small resource-poor country of Palestine into a modern economy. But the inflow of immigrants was accompanied by an inflow of foreign funds—mostly immigrant transfers and private investment, but also large institutional transfers—which financed a persistent balance-of-payments deficit. The import surplus permitted a relatively large rate of capital formation in housing, agriculture, and industry. The combination of capital, a skilled labor force, and entrepreneurial ability, especially among the immigrants from Germany from 1932 to 1936, resulted in rapid economic growth.

The economy did not grow evenly. There was a period of depression in 1926-28, an era of very rapid growth in 1932-35, and another period of depression in 1936-39. World War II brought renewed prosperity, primarily as a result of the tremendous demands of the armed forces. During this period income per capita rose rapidly and manufacturing emerged as a major branch of the economy, although it was not able to maintain its relative position in the economy after the war.

To summarize, the situation at the end of the Mandate was as follows: the Jewish population of Palestine of 700,000 was highly skilled and educated; well organized politically, with a reasonably modern economic structure; dedicated to the idea of rapid economic development and absorption of immigrants; and confident of its ability to attain its economic objectives.

Immigration and Economic Growth

The most distinctive feature of the Israeli economy is the tremendous postwar growth in population. Between May 1948 and the end of 1965 the population trebled, reaching 2.6 million. The main source of growth of the Jewish population has been immigration, although the natural increase of about 2 per cent per year is not inconsiderable. The Arab population, growing only fron natural increase, has still been able to maintain its relative position of about 10 per cent of the population, because its natural increase has been 4 per cent. This remarkably high rate results from the combination of the high birth rate associated with less-developed countries and a death rate as low as that found in the more-developed nations.

The most intense period of immigration occurred immediately after independence. Tens of thousands of Jews, who had been held in Cyprus and in the displaced-persons camps in Europe by British anti-immigration policy streamed to Israel. When this source was exhausted, almost entire Jewish communities from Bulgaria, Poland, Hungary, Rumania, and Middle Eastern countries, such as Yemen, Iraq, and Libya, were transferred to Israel. During the three and a half years from May 1948 to the end of 1951, the population doubled.

Zionist policies had been based on the view that immigration affected but was not contingent on economic policy. Now, however, it was found that to absorb such large numbers of immigrants would take time, which in turn meant that there would have to be a temporary halt to immigration in order to let the economy catch up. Consequently, the Jewish Agency changed its immigration policy: whoever wanted to come was still welcome, but the Agency became selective in encouraging and financing immigration. As a result, immigration fell considerably in 1952, practically stopped in 1953 (when there was net emigration), and resumed at a low level in 1954.

Immigration has fluctuated since 1955, but at no time has it approached either relatively or in absolute numbers the dimensions of the early years of mass-immigration. Over these past 12 years, the greatest number of immigrants in any one year was 71,000 in 1957. (This is the gross figure for immigration and does not take into account emigration.) Nevertheless, even during years of relatively low immigration, the increase of

Table 1: Population of Israel, 1948-65
(end-of-year estimate)

Year	Jews	Non-Jews	Total	Increase in Total Population over the Preceding Year	Annual Average Rate of Growth of Total Population[a]
	(thousands)			(percentage)	
1948	758.7	156.0[b]	914.7		
1949	1,013.9	160.0	1,173.9	28.3	
1950	1,203.0	167.0	1,370.1	16.7	19.9
1951	1,404.4	173.4	1,577.8	15.2	
1952	1,450.2	179.3	1,629.5	3.3	
1953	1,483.6	185.8	1,669.4	2.4	2.9
1954	1,526.0	191.8	1,717.8	2.9	
1955	1,590.5	198.6	1,789.1	4.2	
1956	1,667.5	204.9	1,872.4	4.7	4.8
1957	1,762.7	213.1	1,976.0	5.5	
1958	1,810.1	221.5	2,031.7	2.8	
1959	1,858.8	229.8	2,088.7	2.8	2.9
1960	1,911.2	239.2	2,150.4	3.0	
1960	1,910.8	243.3	2,154.1	—	
1961	1,981.7	252.5	2,234.2	3.7	
1962	2,068.9	262.9	2,331.8	4.4	
1963	2,155.6	274.5	2,430.1	4.2	3.8
1964	2,239.2	286.4	2,525.6	3.9	
1965	2,299.1	299.3	2,598.4	2.9	

Notes: Estimates above the line are based on the Registration of November 8th, 1948; below-the-line estimates are based on the Census of May 22nd, 1961.
[a]Compounded annual average rate of growth. Total increase from 1948 to 1965 is 184 per cent for total population and 203 per cent for Jews.
[b]Estimate for November 8th, 1948 of population within borders of Israel fixed by the 1949 Armistice agreements. (Jewish population at this date was 716,700.)
Sources: Central Bureau of Statistics, *Statistical Abstract of Israel 1966*, No. 17, p. 20, Table B/1; permanent population in 1960 from *Statistical Abstract of Israel 1964*, No. 15, p. 12, Table B/1.

population (including natural increase) has been very high by any international comparison, as can be seen in Table 1.

The growth of population has created economic problems of a fundamental nature at the same time that it has been a positive factor in growth. Immigrants must be cared for, particularly when they are not well off, as has generally been the case in Israel. Basic needs such as food and clothing must be supplied, and so must shelter, which is more expensive. Despite great efforts to expand building activity, fully one-fifth of the population at the end of 1951 was living in temporary and inadequate housing. Even though it is true that these temporary homes were better accomodation than many immigrants had enjoyed before, nevertheless the new arrivals had come to Israel in the expectation of finding decent housing. To supply this was a formidable task.

Even more important in the long run has been the continuing need to provide employment. Unless immigration is to reduce the per capita income, immigrants must find employment at least as productive as the national average. This requires a very high rate of investment.

Economic Growth

Real national product has grown very rapidly over the entire period, with the annual rate of increase in gross national product (GNP) averaging 11.1 per cent from 1950 to 1965. In the early years the growth rate was uneven. The increase in GNP was very rapid in 1951 and 1954 and very slight in 1952 and 1953. Between 1955 and 1965 the rate of growth was steadier, but in 1966 there was hardly any growth at all.

Since population grew so rapidly, the over-all rate of growth in GNP is less meaningful than the growth in per capita GNP. Both series are shown in Table 2. It will be seen that there was actually a decrease in the per capita growth rate in 1952 and 1953. However, despite this there was a substantial average annual increase of 6.3 per cent. Taking this as the most acceptable single measure of economic development, the conclusion is that Israel maintained a fairly steady and rapid rate of growth

Table 2: Growth of Gross National Product, 1950-65
(in constant 1955 prices)

Year	Index (1955 = 100) Aggregate	Index (1955 = 100) Per capita	Per Cent Increase over Preceding Year Aggregate	Per Cent Increase over Preceding Year Per capita
1950	51.4	71.0	–	–
1951	67.2	78.8	30.9	11.0
1952	72.2	78.7	7.4	−0.1
1953	73.1	77.5	1.2	−1.5
1954	89.1	92.4	21.9	19.2
1955	100.0	100.0	12.2	8.2
1956	108.6	103.9	8.6	3.9
1957	118.5	107.4	9.1	3.3
1958	129.6	113.4	9.4	5.6
1959	146.7	124.5	13.2	9.8
1960	168.5	131.1	8.1	5.3
1961	175.3	140.1	10.6	6.9
1962	198.0	151.3	12.9	8.0
1963	220.9	162.5	11.6	7.3
1964	243.7	172.1	10.4	5.9
1965	260.4	177.6	6.8	3.2

Source: Computed from Table 7 and average population figures given in sources for Table 1.

between 1954 and 1966. It is worth mentioning that the distribution of income in Israel is relatively egalitarian, although there has been a tendency toward greater income differentials.[2]

Making international comparisons of levels of real income is complicated by the need to use rates of exchange for converting local currency values into some international unit.[3] Nonetheless, assuming that the official rate of exchange in 1962 was a reasonable one, Israel's per capita income was about $700 in that year; this was far above most of the poorer countries of the world, well above Italy, and better than 60 per cent of the levels for France, West Germany, and the United Kingdom.

---

2. See G. Hanoch, "Income Differentials in Israel," *Fifth Report 1959 and 1960* (Jerusalem: Falk Project for Economic Research in Israel 1961).
3. Thus, for example, the devaluation of the Israeli pound from $1 = 1.80 to $1 = 3.00 in February 1962 suggests that Israel's per capita income dropped from 1961 to 1962, when the official exchange rate is used to convert the figures to dollars. In Tables 6 and 7, effective exchange rates are used to convert imports and exports to local currency values.

Another indicator of the level of development is the industrial origin of national product. This is shown in Table 3. It is quite clear that the high concentration in agriculture associated with underdeveloped countries was absent from the beginning of the period; in fact, it was absent in pre-state Jewish

Table 3: Industrial Origin of Net Domestic Products[a]:
Selected Years (in per cent)

	1952	1955	1958	1961	1963	1965
Agriculture, forestry, fishing	11.4	11.3	13.2	11.1	10.4	8.5
Manufacturing, mining, quarrying	21.7	22.5	22.1	24.7	24.5	24.2
Contract construction	9.2	8.4	8.1	7.5	8.2	7.2
Public utilities	1.7	1.7	2.0	2.2	2.0	2.0
Transport and communication	7.4	7.4	7.7	8.0	8.1	8.8
Finance, insurance, real estate	2.5	2.7	3.0	4.1	4.7	5.0
Ownership of dwellings	5.2	5.4	5.5	6.0	6.8	7.5
Government and private non-profit institutions	18.2	20.0	19.0	18.1	17.2	18.7
Trade and other services	22.7	20.6	19.4	18.3	18.1	18.1
Total	100.0	100.0	100.0	100.0	100.0	100.0

[a]NDP at factor cost before adjustment for inventory changes and depreciation.
Sources: Central Bureau of Statistics, *Statistical Abstract of Israel 1966*, No. 17, pp. 176-77, Table F/15. Construction and public utilities are combined in the above source; they have been segregated here according to Central Bureau of Statistics, *Israel's National Income and Expenditure (1950-1962)*, Special Series No. 153, Jerusalem, 1964 (1952-59) and according to Bank of Israel *Annual Report 1965*, p. 25, Table II-9 (1960-65).

Palestine. This reflects the fact that the Jewish population was transplanted and that the Palestine economy was an open one, relying to a great extent on foreign trade. Equally striking is the high concentration in the total of service items (i.e., activities other than agriculture, manufacturing, and construction). Moreover, manufacturing has had a gradually rising share of the total. More detailed data shows an increasing interdependence among the various sectors of the economy as measured by sales of intermediate goods.[4]

The growth of income is primarily related to inputs of factors of production. First of these is labor. The growth of population increased the supply of labor, but changes in income per capita are not necessarily proportional to changes in product per worker. The altered composition of the population also brought about changes in labor force participation, as can be seen in Table 4. Mass immigration and armed hostilities were reflected in a very low participation rate in 1949, when the civilian labor force comprised about 30 per cent of the total population. This has gradually increased: the labor force now comprises about 35 per cent of the population. However, this is still too low when compared to most developed countries. The situation is explained in part by the rather large fraction of the population under 14 years of age. But there are also low participation rates in three other groups: the 14–17 age group, men over 55, and women who have emigrated from Africa or other parts of Asia. The participation rate of the last two groups has risen in recent years of high employment; that of the 14–17 age group has not declined, even though the per cent attending school has risen.

Throughout most of the period, unemployment was a greater problem than the low participation rate of the labor force. Mass-immigration and demobilization swelled the ranks of the unemployed to a peak of 14 per cent of the labor force in 1949.[5] The disinflationary policy of 1952 and 1953 caused a temporary set-back to the trend of decreasing unemployment. Then from 1954 through 1964, unemployment gradually declined, ceasing to be a major problem; what unemployment remained was largely frictional or structural.[6] However, this

---

4. M. Bruno, *Interdependence, Resource Use and Structural Change in Israel* (Jerusalem: Bank of Israel, 1962).
5. The statistics generally exclude the occupants of immigrant camps from both the labor force and the unemployed; here, however, they are included in both.
6. In this period, these two types of unemployment—frictional and structural—remained at a somewhat higher rate than that for some western European countries. This was due in part to the impact of immigration on Israel and also to the pockets of unemployment arising from limited geographic mobility, reflecting in some degree the government policy of population dispersal.

Table 4: Civilian Labor Force and Unemployment, 1949-65
(in thousands)

Years	Labor Force Total (1)	Labor Force Employed (2)	Labor Force Unemployed (3)	Potential Labor Force in Immigrant Camps (4)	Labor Force plus Potential Total (1)+(4) (5)	Labor Force plus Potential Unemployed (3)+(4) (6)	Unemployment as a percentage of: Labor Force (3)÷(1) (7)	Unemployment as a percentage of: Labor Force plus Potential (6)÷(5) (8)
1949	343	310	33	17	360	50	9.5%	13.9%
1950	450	419	31	22	472	53	6.9	11.2
1951	545	512	33	12	557	45	6.1	8.1
1952	584	542	42	6	590	48	7.2	8.1
1953	599	531	67	2	601	69	11.1	11.3
1954	608	554	54	2	610	56	8.9	9.2
1955	619	573	46				7.4	
1956	646	595	51				7.8	
1957	690	642	48				6.9	
1958	698	658	40				5.7	
1959	714	675	39				5.5	
1960	736	702	34				4.6	
1961	774	746	28				3.6	
1962	818	788	30				3.7	
1963	840	810	30				3.6	
1964	884	854	30				3.3	
1965	912	879	33				3.6	

Sources: 1949-56: A. Hovne, *The Labor Force in Israel*, pp. 12 and 82.
1957-61: Central Bureau of Statistics, *Labour Force Surveys 1955-61*, Special Series No. 162, Jerusalem, 1964, pp. 2 and 4.
1962: Central Bureau of Statistics, *Statistical Abstract of Israel 1963*, No. 14, pp. 486 and 488.
1963-65: Central Bureau of Statistics, *Statistical Abstract of Israel 1966*, No. 17, pp. 290 and 292.

picture has been dimmed by the recession that started in late 1965, which began increasing the ranks of the unemployed in 1966, making unemployment once again a major issue in Israel.

Labor is not a homogenous factor of production: workers differ in ability, attitude toward work, and occupation. Although no statistics are available for measuring skills, there is a presumption in favor of associating skill and productivity with level of education. The average level of education of the Jews of Palestine was very high; it has been estimated that the per cent of the population with college education in 1948 was as high as in the United States and was much higher than in any other country.[7] This was due to the fact that the pre-1948 immigration included a very large number of professional and highly educated people, mostly from central and eastern Europe. The mass-immigration that began in 1948 consisted of far less-educated people: the average educational level among immigrants from Asia and Africa was lower than from Europe and America, and immigrants from Asia and Africa were a much larger fraction of total immigration than before. Furthermore, even among European immigrants, the average level was below that of immigrants from the same countries before the war. Thus, by 1952 the average level of education had dropped, though since 1954 this trend has been stopped and may possibly have reversed. Immigration in recent years has included a larger percentage of people with higher education, and the local educational system has played a more important role, particularly since the institution of compulsory primary education in 1954. Nonetheless, in 1961, 36 per cent of the population age 15 and over had not completed eight years of schooling.[8]

The widespread emphasis on adult education, formal and informal, has compensated partly for the drop in the level of education. The instruction of immigrants in agricultural settlements and widespread adult Hebrew classes have been particularly important in facilitating adjustment to the new country.

Table 5 presents estimates of the structure of Jewish employment, according to major economic sectors. The data do not show any sizable changes over time, although the share of agriculture has declined while that of manufacturing has risen somewhat in recent years. However, the figures do not indicate the extent of occupational mobility that has been present. Immigrants employed abroad in professional, technical, administrative, and commercial positions have tended to switch to agricultural and industrial pursuits after immigration. This general movement

---

7. Using data on veteran (pre-1948) population 30 years and older from the 1954 Labor Force Survey, R. E. Easterlin has estimated the level of education in 1948. "Israel's Development, Past Accomplishments and Future Problems," *Quarterly Journal of Economics*, LXXV (February 1961).
8. Central Bureau of Statistics, *Statistical Abstract of Israel 1961*, No. 12.

Table 5: Structure of Jewish Employment, Selected Years
(per cent of total)

Year	Agriculture	Industry[a]	Construction	Transportation	Commerce	Public Services	Personal Services	Total	Total in Thousands
1936	21.4	20.1	9.4	5.3	15.7	18.1	10.0	100.0	156.5
1945	13.4	31.1	4.9	5.1	14.7	20.8	10.0	100.0	233.2
1947[b]	12.6	26.5	8.7	6.3	19.4[b]	18.6	7.9	100.0	253.0
1948	14.2	31.8	6.1	6.2	13.3	18.9	9.5	100.0	311.8
1951[b]	13.8	23.6	9.5	7.0	16.8[b]	18.2	11.1	100.0	505.0
1954	14.7	24.5	9.2	6.7	13.1	21.8	10.0	100.0	474.4
1955	15.0	23.7	9.1	6.4	14.0	23.1	8.7	100.0	542.3
1959	14.2	25.6	9.2	6.8	12.4	24.0	7.8	100.0	627.8
1961	14.5	25.6	8.5	6.7	12.3	25.0	7.4	100.0	687.7
1963[c]	11.5	27.7[d]	9.3	7.2	13.4	23.2	7.7	100.0	743.1
1965[c]	11.0	28.0	9.5	7.0	13.0	23.8	7.7	100.0	810.5

[a] Includes electricity and national water supply.
[b] Includes income recipients other than employed persons; mainly affects "Commerce."
[c] These figures have not been adjusted for uniformity with the data on earlier years.
[d] Includes public utilities.

Sources: All years except 1963 and 1965: Gur Ofer, *The Services in a Developing Economy: Israel as a Case Study* (Jerusalem: Bank of Israel and New York: Frederick A. Praeger, 1967) p. 88, Tables 4 and 6. 1963 and 1965: Central Bureau of Statistics, *Statistical Abstract of Israel 1966*, No. 17, p. 304, Table K/11.

was particularly observable prior to 1948, and it has continued since then, though to a lesser degree. But the veteran population has tended to shift back into the types of employment for which they were trained abroad.[9] Thus, there may have been some tendency to make more use of the existing stock of education, even while the general average dropped.

Studies on productivity in Israel are subject to considerable reservation on both theoretical and empirical grounds, but there appears to have been a substantial increase in productivity between 1950 and 1963. According to the best available estimates, the average annual rate of increase in productivity during these years was between 2.2 and 2.7 per cent.[10] Although the increase in output per worker is a great achievement considering the intrinsic difficulty of absorbing the large increase in labor input, it is clear that the main contribution to the increase in output per worker is the increase in capital inputs.

Fixed reproducible capital per worker increased at an average annual rate of about 8 per cent, a very rapid rate considering the rate of growth of labor inputs.[11] Table 6, which shows indexes of growth of the various components of total resources, presents figures on the growth of capital formation. Table 7 shows the allocation of total resources, in current prices. The share of gross capital formation was quite high, ranging from 22 to 27 per cent. What is also clear from the table is that domestic saving—defined as gross national product *minus* public consumption, private consumption, and depreciation—was zero or negative during most of the period. In other words, a high level of investment was made possible by the persistent and sizable import surplus, which is seen in Table 6. Next to the growth of population, this large import surplus (or capital inflow in the balance-of-payments sense) is perhaps the most distinctive feature of the Israeli economy.

---

9. Figures on these trends can be found in Central Bureau of Statistics publications: *Census of Population 1948* and *Labor Force Survey, 1954*.
10. The basic study on productivity is A. L. Gaathon, *Capital, Employment and Output in Israel 1950–1959* (Jerusalem: Bank of Israel, 1961). The figures given are revised estimates by Gaathon.
11. *Ibid*. This figure excludes housing, which accounts for close to two-fifths of all fixed capital.

Table 6: Resources at the Disposal of the Economy and Their Uses,[a] 1950-66
(per cent)

Year	Consumption Private	Consumption Public	Depreciation	Net Domestic Capital Formation	Use of Resources at Disposal of the Economy	GNP	Import Surplus	Resources at Disposal of Economy
1950	59.2	16.0	3.1	21.7	100.0	79.5	20.5	100.0
1951	57.1	15.5	3.3	24.1	100.0	82.7	17.3	100.0
1952	58.8	14.7	5.2	21.3	100.0	77.7	22.3	100.0
1953	61.1	14.9	6.6	17.4	100.0	78.4	21.6	100.0
1954	61.4	14.8	6.8	17.0	100.0	79.8	20.2	100.0
1955	58.2	15.8	6.4	19.6	100.0	78.7	21.3	100.0
1956	57.0	20.5	6.5	16.0	100.0	77.7	22.3	100.0
1957	58.5	16.8	6.9	17.8	100.0	80.2	19.8	100.0
1958	59.6	16.2	6.8	17.4	100.0	81.8	18.2	100.0
1959	59.8	16.1	6.8	17.3	100.0	84.6	15.4	100.0
1960	60.2	16.1	7.1	16.6	100.0	84.9	15.1	100.0
1961	58.4	16.5	7.0	18.1	100.0	84.0	16.0	100.0
1962	55.8	17.5	7.7	19.0	100.0	80.3	19.7	100.0
1963	57.4	17.2	8.2	17.2	100.0	82.4	17.6	100.0
1964	56.6	16.3	7.9	19.2	100.0	80.6	19.4	100.0
1965	58.6	17.9	8.2	15.3	100.0	83.5	16.5	100.0
1966	61.2	19.6	8.5	10.7	100.0	85.8	14.2	100.0

[a]Computed in current prices.

Sources: 1950-65: Central Bureau of Statistics, *Statistical Abstract of Israel 1966*, No. 17, pp. 156-57, Table F/1. 1966: Central Bureau of Statistics, "Preliminary Estimates of the National Accounts 1966," *Statistical Bulletin of Israel*, XVIII (Supplements, January 1967), p. 18. The export and import figures have been adjusted by use of "effective exchange rates" rather than official rates.

Table 7: Real Resources and Their Uses, 1950-66[a]

(index: 1955 = 100)

Year	Consumption			Domestic Capital Formation			Use of Resources at Disposal of Economy	Exports	Total Use of Resources	Imports	GNP
	Private	Public	Total	Gross	Net	Depreciation					
1950	58.9	64.3	60.1	85.7	99.4	43.7	66.8	35.7	64.1	96.4	51.4
1951	72.2	76.2	73.1	101.3	118.0	50.0	80.4	43.8	77.2	102.7	67.2
1952	77.6	72.0	76.4	87.0	93.1	68.4	79.2	59.3	77.4	90.8	72.2
1953	80.4	75.2	79.3	72.8	70.2	81.0	77.6	74.8	77.3	88.2	73.1
1954	92.4	87.9	91.4	81.2	76.9	94.3	88.8	102.7	90.0	92.1	89.1
1955	100.0	100.0	100.0	100.0	100.0	100.0	100.0	100.0	100.0	100.0	100.0
1956	109.1	143.9	116.5	94.6	89.3	110.9	110.8	114.3	111.1	117.7	108.6
1957	116.9	122.4	118.0	110.7	106.0	125.3	116.1	137.2	118.0	116.7	118.5
1958	128.7	125.7	128.1	119.0	113.3	136.2	125.7	152.7	128.0	124.0	129.6
1959	141.5	130.1	139.1	130.0	123.5	150.0	136.7	200.0	142.2	130.8	146.7
1960	151.0	138.8	148.4	138.0	128.3	167.8	145.7	251.9	154.9	145.8	158.5
1961	167.7	163.8	166.8	163.5	156.7	184.5	166.0	291.8	176.9	181.0	175.3
1962	186.0	182.5	185.2	183.7	173.0	216.7	184.9	351.9	199.3	202.9	198.0
1963	204.4	194.6	202.3	190.1	171.1	248.3	199.1	413.9	217.8	209.7	220.9
1964	226.5	204.2	221.7	231.0	217.1	273.6	224.1	444.9	243.3	241.9	243.7
1965	245.4	226.4	241.3	216.7	187.2	306.9	234.9	484.1	256.5	246.6	260.4
1966	237.9	237.9	250.9	187.8	138.5	339.1	234.5	533.3	260.4	250.3	264.4
						Annual rate of growth compounded (per cent)				
1950-65	4.2	3.5	4.0	2.5	1.9	7.0	3.5	13.6	4.0	2.6	5.1

[a]Computed in current prices.
Source: See Table 6.

Capital Inflow

Israel's annual balance of payments in dollar terms from 1949 to 1965, is summarized in Table 8.[12] Exports of goods and services have increased at an annual rate of growth of about 15 per cent since 1952. The growth has consisted of the expansion of citrus exports (the main export item of Palestine) and the development of industrial and service exports. The principal industrial export is cut and polished diamonds, but in recent years there has been considerable diversification, with exports of clothing, plywood, processed foods, and metal products growing both absolutely and relatively. The important and expanding service items are sea and air transport and tourism.

Imports too have increased considerably, at an average annual rate of about 10 per cent since 1952; but there have been considerable annual fluctuations, with imports actually decreasing in two consecutive years, 1952 and 1953, and barely rising in 1954, 1958, and again in 1966. The composition of merchandise imports has changed, with raw materials and semi-finished goods increasing relatively to finished consumer goods. The chief service imports are transportation, interest charges, and other government foreign exchange expenditures, including those for defense.

Exports have risen faster than imports, increasing from only 22 per cent of imports in 1952 to 6 per cent in 1965. However, the import surplus has tended to increase, although wide annual fluctuations are noticeable. In the earlier years it ranged between $250–350 million, while more recently the range has been $400–450 million. In 1964 the import surplus reached the unprecedented figure of $569 million, but declined in 1965 and 1966.

A balance-of-payments deficit, by definition, implies that sources were available for its financing. But the type of financing is important for evaluating the future burden of present deficits. In the early years, the import surplus necessitated drawings on the previously accumulated sterling balances. Gradually,

---

12. It should be pointed out that the estimates prior to 1952 are not reliable.

Table 8:   Balance of Payments, 1949-65
(in millions of U. S. dollars)

Year	Current Account[a] Credit	Current Account[a] Debit	Current Account[a] Net Credit	Unilateral Transfers Net Credit	Long-term Capital Net Credit	Short-term Capital Net Credit	Errors and Omissions Net Credit
1949	43	263	−220	118	43	24	35
1950	46	328	−282	90	68	51	73
1951	67	426	−359	137	133	32	57
1952	86	393	−307	191	115	1	− 0
1953	102	365	−263	173	69	6	15
1954	135	373	−238	261	71	− 70	−24
1955	144	427	−283	210	76	0	− 3
1956	178	535	−357	241	78	22	16
1957	222	557	−335	245	70	9	11
1958	235	569	−334	264	67	− 1	4
1959	286	602	−316	251	80	− 25	9
1960	359	696	−337	311	101	− 60	−15
1961	425	857	−432	346	176	− 72	−18
1962	503	958	−455	331	203	−105	26
1963	607	1,011	−404	347	171	− 98	−16
1964[b]	656	1,225	−569	351	275	− 48	− 9
1965[b]	750	1,271	−521	341	248	− 29	−39
1949-65	4,844	10,856	−6,011	4,208	2,044	−363	122

[a]Based on recording of exports f.o.b. and imports c.i.f.
[b]Services debit includes expenditures abroad of the national institutions.
Sources: 1949: M. Michaely, *Foreign Trade and Capital Imports in Israel* (Tel Aviv: AmOved, 1963; Hebrew), p. 58, Table 25.
1950-54: N. Halevi, *Estimates of Israel's International Transactions: 1952-54* (Jerusalem: Falk Project, 1956), as quoted in slightly corrected form by Don Patinkin, *The Israel Economy: The First Decade* (Jerusalem: Falk Project, 1960), p. 52, Table 16.
1955-65 (A): *Bulletin*, Part 8 (economic statistics) XVII (March 1966), p. 342 (for 1955-62); Bank of Israel, *Annual Report 1964*, p. 35, Table III-I (for 1963) and *Annual Report 1965*, p. 39, Table III-3 (for 1964-65).
1958-65 (B): *Abstract 1963*, No. 14, p. 407, Table (for 1959); *Abstract 1965*, No. 16, p. 223, Table H/1 (for 1958, 1960-61); *Bulletin* (March 1966), *loc. cit.* (for 1962-63); *Bulletin*, XVIII (March 1967), p. 48 (for 1964-65). Some of the figures from the *Abstracts* have been adjusted for minor corrections in later *Bulletins*.

unilateral transfers, loans, and investments were developed. Since 1959, these long-term capital inflows have been larger than the annual deficit on current account, and have enabled substantial foreign exchange reserves to be built up.

Table 9: Main Sources of Long-term Capital Inflow, 1949-65
(in millions of U. S. dollars)

Year	World Jewry Unilateral Transfers (1)	World Jewry Long-term[b] Capital Transfers (2)	World Jewry Total (1)+(2) (3)	World Jewry Total (3) as Per Cent of Import Surplus (4)	U. S. Government Unilateral Transfers (5)	U. S. Government Long-term[d] Capital Transfers (6)	U. S. Government Total (5)+(6) (7)	U. S. Government Total (7) as Per Cent of Import Surplus (8)	West Germany[a] Unilateral Transfers (9)	West Germany[a] Total (9) as Per Cent of Import Surplus (10)
1949	118	25	143	65	—	18	18	8	—	—
1950	90	21	111	39	—	44	44	16	—	—
1951	123	97	220	61	14	28	42	12	—	—
1952	105	81	186	61	86	28	114	37	—	—
1953	85	65	150	57	47	4	51	19	41	16
1954	133	57	190	80	39	2	41	17	88	37
1955	83	48	131	46	21	23	44	16	106	38
1956	128	65	193	54	7	30	37	10	105	29
1957	98	64	162	48	24	9	33	10	123	37
1958	112	47	159	48	16	13	29	9	135	40
1959	104	61	165	53	9	20	29	9	137	43
1960	123	82	205	61	14	21	35	10	174	51
1961	137	92	229	53	10	22	32	7	199	46
1962	142	122	264	58	8	31	39	9	181	40
1963	173	176	349	86	6	32	38	9	167	41
1964	192	170[e]	362	64	8	42	50	9	151	26
1965	206	131[e]	337	65	5	52	57	11	129	25
1949-65	2,152	1,404	3,556	59	314	419	733	12	1,736	22

[a]Includes restitutions and reparations. Unilateral transfers only, since there are no separate figures for loans.
[b]Some of the net private foreign investment included here is undoubtedly from non-Jews.
[c]Grants and technical assistance.
[d]All loans from United States government agencies, including Export-Import Bank.
[e]Net of investment abroad by Israel.

Sources: Computed from references listed for Table 8.

The long-term capital inflow thus made the persistent deficit possible. Since fully 70 per cent of the deficit for the period as a whole was covered by unilateral transfers, the burden accumulated for future repayment was relatively small. Nevertheless, annual capital charges (excluding principal repayment) amounted to 13 per cent of gross export earnings in 1964.[13]

Three major sources of capital inflow may be distinguished: World Jewry, the United States government, and West Germany. Table 9 shows the annual inflow from these sources from 1949 to 1965.

World Jewry

World Jewry is the main supplier of funds to Israel. Over the 1949-65 period, World Jewry accounted for slightly more than half of all unilateral transfers to Israel and nearly 70 per cent of the long-term capital flowing in from abroad.

Among the unilateral transfers, institutional transfers are of particular importance. To supplement these, an organization for the sale of State of Israel Bonds abroad was set up in 1951. Sales of bonds up to April 1966 amounted to $850 million, of which $350 million were redeemed, mostly in local currency for use in Israel. These bonds presently account for some two-fifths of all Israel's foreign exchange debts.[14]

Private investment from abroad increased rapidly during the 1960's. Not all of these funds are from Jewish sources; but since most are, no great error arises from including the entire sum under this heading. Although all types of Jewish transfers to Israel reflect strong sentimental influence, there is a clear tendency toward greater reliance on economic consideration. As shown in Table 9, the various net transfers of long-term funds by World Jewry have exceeded those from any other source in all but one year (1950), and have financed 58 per cent of the import surplus of the period as a whole.

---

13. Net capital charges (i.e., interest payments minus receipts) amounted to only 9 per cent of export earnings exclusive of interest receipts.
14. *Summary of Foreign Exchange Accounts for Fiscal Year 1965/66,* Ministry of Finance, Jerusalem, 1966 (in Hebrew) pp. 45-46.

United States Government

The first type of United States aid to Israel was a $100 million Export-Import Bank Loan approved in 1949, although this is not an integral part of what is commonly defined as economic assistance. In 1951, Israel was added to the list of countries receiving economic assistance, and during the next three years grants were substantial. In the course of time, United States aid switched in emphasis from grants to soft-currency loans (under various aid and agricultural surplus programs), and in recent years some shift to hard-currency loans is apparent. Military aid was excluded from the various programs. Since 1956, United States aid of all kinds has been generally less than $40 million a year.

West Germany

In 1952, the Federal Republic of Germany signed a Reparations Agreement which stipulated payment of over $800 million during a twelve-year period, almost entirely in German goods, except for fuel. In 1954, restitution payments to individuals were added. Gradually, reparation payments declined, ending in 1965, and restitutions rose to some $140 million per year. Since 1954, Germany has been the second largest source of capital inflow. Although newspaper accounts have mentioned other kinds of German aid, no additional funds are so designated in the published accounts. There are indications, however, that some long-term loans are replacing the Reparations Agreement.

The capital inflow served two main functions: it provided scarce foreign exchange and, as already stressed, increased total resources which could be allocated for various purposes. Some of the capital inflow was "tied," in the sense that it placed restrictions on the types and sources of imports. Also, much of the capital inflow was "tied" in the sense that it entailed commitment to specific allocation of resources. For example, institutional transfers of the Jewish Agency were designed to provide for the immediate needs of immigrants—for their housing and for land settlement; such transfers thus went either for public consumption[15] or for investment.

Similarly, the counterpart funds of United States aid had to go to investment in projects approved by the United States Operations Mission in Israel. In most cases, such tied aid was not really necessary, for Israel was quite committed—without outside pressure—to an ambitious investment program; it was therefore not difficult to find projects among those considered in the government's Development Budget that would meet the approval of the U.S.O.M. This is not to say that the two-party investment discussions never affected investment decision; they certainly affected the manner in which projects were evaluated. There were indirect effects as well; e.g., the way in which the Israel Industrial Development Bank was set up and the form of its operations were the results of negotiations in connnection with United States financial assistance for that institution.

German reparations constitute an interesting special case. Fears that the agreement might not be fulfilled—these, of course, have since proved groundless—created a sense of urgency in utilizing the funds. Many projects were undertaken that might otherwise have been postponed or even rejected, such as the massive build-up of the merchant navy.

In sum, the capital inflow financed not only investment but also consumption, since for the period as a whole domestic savings were negative.[16] As shown above, some transfers were earmarked for consumption, but this has no bearing on the allocation of total resources between consumption and investment. That the availability of foreign aid lessened the need to mobilize domestic savings is obvious. It is less clear whether, given the amount and forms of available capital inflow, efforts

---

15. The public sector in Israel is made up of the government, the National Institution, and the local authorities.
16. The traditional method of classifying "investment" and "consumption" is misleading; much of the public consumption and even part of the private consumption by new immigrants in the early years were really investments in human resources.

should have been made to increase domestic savings and investment, or to reduce the import surplus.[17]

Economic Policy

As mentioned earlier, responsibility for initiating development in the Jewish sector during the Mandate was accepted by the chief Jewish national institutions: the Jewish Agency for Palestine, the Jewish National Fund, and the World Zionist Organization. The main economic activities of these institutions were raising funds abroad, directing immigration, buying land, and setting up agricultural settlements. Other institutions dealt with health, education, and other social services. The labor movement—combining Zionist and social ideology—also took upon itself much more than just trade union activities. The Histadrut (the General Federation of Jewish Labor) provided many welfare services and initiated economic activity through both cooperatives and companies directed by a central holding company.

Once independence was achieved it was natural that the central government would assume primary responsibility for economic development. Many functions of the national institutions were transferred to the government, but not all; for example, the Jewish Agency still deals with immigration and land settlement. Similarly, even among the socialist parties there are differences of opinion concerning the suitable roles respectively of the government and the Histadrut.

The Tools of Policy

Two types of public economic policy must be distinguished: direct activity and the influencing of the decisions of the non-

---
17. See, e.g., D. Patinkin, *The Israel Economy: The First Decade* (Jerusalem: Falk Project for Economic Research in Israel, 1960), chapter 5.

public sectors. Direct activity includes production or purchase by publicly controlled economic units. Estimates have been made of the sectoral structure of net product and employment.[18] In 1959, the public sector accounted for 21.6 per cent of net domestic product and 24 per cent of employment. The product share is not unusually high compared to some Western European countries, although the employment share is. Moreover, the Histadrut sector accounted for 20.3 per cent of net domestic product and some 21 per cent of employment. Thus the residual "private sector," at less than 60 per cent of product and employment, is much smaller than in other non-communist countries. On the other hand, there does not seem to have been any significant change over time in the shares of the various sectors.[19]

The public sector's purchases of goods and services as a per cent of GNP (25 per cent in 1959), its share of gross investment (53 per cent in 1959), and public consumption as a per cent of resources, are quite high for a country with Israel's per capita income level. Barkai attributes this primarily to ideological considerations,[20] but no less important is the fact that the tremendous capital inflow went predominantly to the public sector. This also largely accounts for the high level of employment in the public sector.[21]

No less important than direct economic activity has been the public influence on private activity. These influences have included direct controls and financial inducements.

The major instruments of policy have been the following:
The State budget. Government receipts include taxes, local loans,

---

18. H. Barkai, "The Public, Histadrut and Private Sectors in the Israel Economy," *Sixth Report 1961-1963* (Jerusalem: Falk Project for Economic Research in Israel, 1964). Classification by sector is highly arbitrary; Barkai's classification is by ownership of voting shares, so that the product of a company owned 50 per cent or more by the public sector is attributed wholly to that sector.
19. H. Barkai, *op. cit.*, compares his own estimates with those for 1953 prepared by D. Creamer in *Israel's National Income: 1950-54*, Falk Project for Economic Research in Israel and Central Bureau of Statistics, Jerusalem, 1957.
20. *Ibid.* pp. 72-73.
21. The over-concentration of employment in public services and the role of the capital inflow in explaining this are discussed by Gur Ofer in *The Service Industries in the Israel Economy*.

and foreign grants and loans. All but the first have been used to finance investment activity, both the direct public activities mentioned above and loans and grants to the nonpublic sectors. Public financing of investment activity has ranged between 40–80 per cent of total gross capital formation.[22]

Particular projects, such as agricultural settlement, water resources, export industries, and industries in "development areas," have received preferential treatment through larger loans or grants and favorable interest rates and terms of repayment.

Taxes have been used not only to finance public consumption, but as a means of affecting income distribution, the allocation of private expenditure, and investment. Taxes on imports have been a major tool of foreign exchange policy.

Foreign Exchange Control. Foreign exchange control, instituted during World War II, has been retained ever since. The controls consist of the licensing of all foreign exchange expenditures and obligatory sale to authorized dealers of foreign exchange receipts. An annual Foreign Exchange Budget determines priorities in licensing, although the tendency in recent years to liberalize imports has done much to convert this budget from a licensing plan to a forecast of expenditures.

During most of the period, a multiple exchange rate system has been in effect, employing the use either of several formal rates or of multiple "effective rates" achieved by taxing foreign exchange expenditures and subsidizing receipts. On the expenditure side, multiple rates have been used to curb expenditures according to some system of bureaucratically determined priorities, to encourage import-substitution, and to manipulate prices of commodities of importance to the cost-of-living index. On the receipt side, multiple rates have been employed to encourage various types of exports and often to discriminate against those foreign exchange receipts the amounts of which were believed

---

22. The percentage varies according to the definition of public financing. In recent years, the ratio has been about 40 per cent, but the apparent decline reflects institutional changes whereby finance of an essentially public nature is channeled through a special institution, e.g., a development bank, and thus is excluded from the budget.

to be independent of the rate of exchange, e.g., most unilateral transfers.

Price Control. During 1949-51, there was widespread control of commodity prices, and throughout the period there have been officially set prices for foreign exchange, rent, and interest rates, and for commodities in the case of approved cartels. In addition, subsidies and persuasion have been used to influence prices. Marketing boards have controlled the production and prices of major agricultural commodities.

Monetary Policy. In the early years, the issuing of currency was subservient to budgetary needs, and monetary curbs were ineffective. In 1954 the Bank of Israel was set up; and it has attempted, with partial success, to limit the expansion of credit, primarily through the use of liquidity ratios, and during the 1953-58 period, through credit ceilings. Exemption from control has been used to channel credit to desired projects.

Wage Policy. Since the Histadrut encompasses about 90 per cent of all wage earners, wage negotiations are pretty much one-sided affairs. But the Histadrut has to a considerable degree accepted responsibility for keeping wages down, particularly since 1960. Thus, the major wage disputes in recent years have been between the Histadrut and various groups of its members who rejected the Histadrut-agreed raises in wages as being too small. An important part of the Wage Bill is an automatic cost-of-living adjustment, and this linking of costs to prices has been a basic source of cost inflation, particularly in 1952-56 and 1961-63.

Planning. In 1949, a four-year development plan was drawn up, but it was virtually ignored by policy makers. Partial plans have been employed throughout in particular sectors where the control by the public sector has been large; e.g., agriculture and housing. Since 1958, encouragement of industry has been carried out in accordance with government plans for industry. Since 1958, attempts have been made to draw up detailed over-all plans, showing the interrelationships between all the sectors of the economy and the role of alternative policy measures. A special Planning Authority was set up. However, to date the most influential economic ministers have not shown readiness to implement this type of economic plan.

The Shifts in Economic Policy

The main aims of economic policy have been the absorption of immigration and the raising of standards of living of the population, both the veterans and the newcomers. In other words, rapid economic development has been a basic policy objective. Of course, there has been constant competition between the satisfaction of immediate needs as against future needs, as for example, between defense and immediate consumption versus investment.

Additional constraints on activities to stimulate growth has been the need to deal with particular problems, often resulting from the investment program; e.g., the balance-of-payments deficit and inflation. Two subsidiary goals of policy affecting the pattern and rate of growth have been the desire to stimulate particular sectors of the economy and the desire to disperse the population. How these objectives and policies have shifted can best be seen by a brief historical examination. From 1949 to 1966, there have been five distinct periods:

1949-51. This was the period of mass immigration. The major problem was how to provide for the immediate needs of the new immigrants—food and shelter—and employment for new immigrants and demobilized soldiers. The inflationary financing of the War of Independence and the expulsion of Palestine (in February 1948) from the Sterling Bloc added to the difficulties.

The solution adopted was an austerity program, which consisted of extensive price controls, and the rationing of food and other necessities, raw materials, and foreign exchange. At the same time, inflationary financing was used to launch an investment program, primarily in building and agricultural settlement. This program was successful in guaranteeing a minimum standard of consumption to everyone, and in diverting an unparalleled share of resources to investment. However, failure to absorb cash balances in the hands of the public—the result of inflationary fiscal policy and inadequate monetary policy—poor administration of the rationing program, and gradual public disillusionment with austerity led to rapid deterioration of the system in 1951. Growing black markets, the discovery that unrealistic relative prices were leading to misallocation of resources, and a severe foreign exchange shortage combined to bring about a reversal of policy toward the end of 1951, but which was officially declared in February 1952.

1952-55. The New Economic Policy consisted of the devaluation of the Israeli pound to three formal rates, with a gradual shifting of commodities from the highest rate of one Israeli pound equals $2.80 to the lowest rate of one pound equals $1, the cessation of "printing press" fiscal policy, and an attempt to control bank credit to the public. At the same time, a more basic decision was taken: to cut down immigration. In other words it was decided that the economy must first absorb the mass-immigration of the previous period, much of which was still unemployed and still living in temporary housing.

The immediate results of the new policy were a decline in real purchasing power of the cash which the community had accumulated, a decline in inflationary pressure (see Table 10), and an improvement in the balance of payments; but this was accompanied by a stagnation of output (and a decline in output per capita) in 1952 and 1953, and an increase of unemployment. The gradual easing of the disinflationary policy in 1953, the readjustment brought about during the recession, and the fruition of previous investments combined to bring about a tremendous rate of growth in 1954 and 1955, during which time unemployment declined markedly. At the same time, new sources of foreign aid were mobilized to consolidate the foreign exchange position, and a new official rate of exchange was adopted: 1.80 Israeli pound = $1. During this period agricultural settlement

Table 10: Money Supply and Cost-of-Living Index,[a] 1948-66

Year	Money Supply[b] Millions of Israeli Pounds	Money Supply[b] Percentage Increase over Previous Year[e]	Cost-of-Living Index 1955 = 100	Cost-of-Living Index Percentage Increase over Previous Year[e]
1948	93[c]	—	38	—
1949	129[d]	38.5	39	2.2
1950	170	31.7	36	− 6.6
1951	224	32.0	42	14.1
1952	247	10.4	66	57.7
1953	290	17.3	84	28.1
1953[a]	263	—	84	—
1954	330	25.8	94	12.2
1955	398	20.5	100	5.9
1956	469	17.9	106	6.4
1957	560	19.4	113	6.5
1958	646	15.2	117	3.4
1959	727	12.5	119	1.5
1960	826	13.7	122	2.3
1961	974	17.9	130	6.7
1962	1,138	16.8	142	9.5
1963	1,489	30.9	151	6.6
1964	1,683	13.0	159	5.2
1965	1,833	9.0	171	7.7
1966	1,967	7.3	185	8.0

[a]Old series figures up to 1953 differ from later series primarily by inclusion of foreign exchange demand deposits.
[b]Money supply includes cash held by public and demand deposits.
[c]Estimated on basis of December 1948 figure.
[d]Average of March-December.
[e]Calculated from less-rounded figures.
Sources: Column 1 1948-1957: D. Patinkin, *The Israel Economy: The First Decade* (Jerusalem: Project for Economic Research, 1960), Table 39. (Based on Central Bureau of Statistics, and Bank of Israel data).
1958-1964: Bank of Israel, *Annual Report 1964*, p. 326.
1965: Bank of Israel, *Annual Report 1965*, p. 318.
1966: Bank of Israel, *Bulletin No. 28*, p. 95.
Column 3 1948-1965: Central Bureau of Statistics, *Statistical Abstract of Israel 1966*, No. 17, p. 273.
1966: Central Bureau of Statistics, *Statistical Bulletin of Israel*, XVIII (March 1967), p. 39.

and production still received primary attention, although attention was also turned to infrastructure investments.

1956-1961. Except for 1956, which was the year of the Sinai campaign, this period was one of fairly steady growth, and declining unemployment.

Immigration fluctuated, but never reached the pre-1952 magnitude. Inflationary pressures declined during 1957-59, and the balance-of-payments deficit was relatively constant. At this time it was realized that agriculture could not be expanded much further; in fact, farm surpluses began to be a serious problem, and price policy had to shift from efforts to set maximum prices to efforts to set minimum prices. Investment in water resources were intensified, and various subsidies were given to raise earnings in agriculture. Increasing attention was devoted to manufacturing in the Government Development Budget, and other efforts were made to encourage manufacturing investment. Immigrants were now taken directly to permanent homes, preferably in new industrial towns in the south and north of the country. Public housing and industrial development policy were used to support the population dispersal, but employment possibilities lagged behind population growth in the "development areas."

Although the foreign exchange position was much improved, efforts were directed toward improving the balance of payments. Various subsidies were given to exports, and a variety of taxes were imposed on imports. The "effective rates" on imports were accompanied by liberalization of licensing. However, when it was believed that a product could be made locally, its production was protected by prohibition of imports. Despite expansion of exports, primarily industrial, the balance-of-payments deficit grew in 1959-61. Capital inflow exceeded the deficit, so that foreign exchange reserves were built up. These, however, greatly increased the money supply and new inflationary pressures arose.

1962-64. In February 1962, a New Economic Policy was once more announced. The pound was devalued to one Israeli pound equals $1. This was designed to improve the balance of payments and to unify the effective exchange rates, which by then had become numerous and complicated. Other clauses of the new policy called for the elimination of administrative protection and the development of competitiveness. Administrative protection was gradually reduced on industrial (but not agricultural) goods, though high initial protective duties prevented any serious dislocation of production.

The average effective exchange rates for exports was only slightly raised by the devaluation, that is exporters received only slightly more per dollar of net foreign exchange receipts than before the devaluation. To prevent the elimination of this slight improvement in the exporter's position, indirect price controls were attempted, with producers of industrial goods "bribed" or coerced by an official Price Staff into keeping down prices. At the same time, the continuous capital inflow, now converted at a higher rate, increased the supply of money considerably. In fact, it was fear of just such inflationary pressure that prevented the adoption of a lower rate in 1962. Fiscal policy and monetary curbs did not prevent the creation of excess demand. Once again, price policy attacked symptoms more than causes. Nonetheless, official intervention in the market kept the Consumer Price Index (and thus wages linked to the cost of living) from rising as much as it otherwise would have in 1962 and 1963; but in 1964 wages rose much more than planned. The results of these indirect controls were steady rises in uncontrolled prices—e.g., land, housing (until 1964), and services—and even more disconcerting, a rise in real purchasing power, which turned into a demand for more imports and competed for exportable goods. Thus, after a slight improvement in the balance of payments in 1963 (following a worsening in 1962), there was a tremendous increase in imports and a relative stagnation of exports in 1964.

1965-1966. Strong anti-inflationary monetary policy adopted late in 1955, uncurbed wage increases, and a sharp decline in immigration and consequent construction activity combined to bring about a severe recession, whose magnitudes grew throughout 1966. Public policy makers maintained that the recession was a tool to transform the economy to meet the requirement of international competition and improve the balance-of-payments position. The balance-of-payments deficit did in fact decline in 1965 and again in 1966. But the idea was to decrease the deficit while maintaining growth; in 1966 there was practically no growth, and investments declined. Moreover, the increase of unemployment among industrial workers raises doubts concerning the achievement of a transformation of the economy. In short, the price paid for the improvement in the balance of payments, in terms of rising unemployment and foregone output, was very high; it remains to be seen whether any permanent benefits were achieved.

Problems and Prospects

The major long-term problem facing the Israeli economy is the gradual decline in foreign economic assistance. Frequently in the past, predictions concerning the impending decline of the capital inflow have proved wrong; the emergence of new sources—German reparations restitutions, private investment—has replaced declining sources. But without venturing to set a date it is clear that the balance-of-payments deficit cannot continue to grow indefinitely, and will have to be cut substantially in the near, if not immediate, future. The fundamental question is not whether the deficit can be cut—by definition, when the capital inflow drops it will be cut—but rather how such a decrease in the import surplus will affect future growth. Will the economy be able to reachieve and maintain its rapid rate of growth when it must rely primarily on domestic saving for investment? Equally important is the question of whether exports can be expanded enough to permit a small deficit at a high level of foreign trade; if not, a shift toward autarky can only decrease economic efficiency.

The answers to these questions depend on what will be done in the interim to make the economy, and particularly manufacturing, more competitive. Until 1966, industry had developed under hot-house conditons; very little had been done to prepare it to do without protection. It is not clear whether the 1966 recession did much to increase competitiveness. Closely connected to these problems is the question of reliance on the market mechanism. Israel today is very much a mixed economy, not only in the sense of the sectoral structure of output, but also in the sense of intricate public intervention in the market, and often administrative intervention. At the moment there are no indications of an imminent shift either toward greater reliance on free market forces or toward a more planned economy.

Appendix

Summary of Positive and Negative Factors

This paper has touched on only some of the factors determining Israel's economic development. Three factors have been stressed: mass immigration in the early years and continuously rapid population growth thereafter; large-scale capital inflow; and public initiative to speed up economic development, financed in part by the capital inflow.

Many other factors besides these have of course influenced Israel's economic growth either negatively or positively, and while some of these have been mentioned briefly in this paper, others have been omitted because of space limitations. To put these many diverse elements into perspective, the author has drawn up a list of the factors that have stimulated or impeded growth. These are presented in parallel columns for the reader's easy reference beginning on the next page.

Factors that Have Stimulated or Impeded Growth

Government

Positive Factors	Negative Factors
Israel has a stable, democratic regime. There is firm acceptance of the idea of economic development and public responsibility for initiating it.	Since Israel is surrounded by hostile neighbors, defense expenditures are relatively high; moreover, the Arab boycott prevents the economy from developing on lines of regional comparative advantage.
An honest and dedicated civil service shows a readiness to adopt new ideas and depart from established norms.	A majority party is lacking, and the coalition governments are unwilling to enter into policy commitments for as much as a year before elections.
	The romantic pre-state era has given an aura of tradition to ideologies, practices, and institutions not necessarily suited for dealing with modern problems.
	The civil service lacks experience and a tradition of public service.
	There is considerable overlapping of functions, among both government agencies and national institutions.

The People

Positive Factors	Negative Factors
The population is young, rapidly growing, generally literate and educated, ready to accept change, and oriented toward a market economy.	Immigration presents pressing problems that encourage short-term rather than long-term solutions.
There is a general acceptance of the goals of economic growth, as well as a recognition of the desirability of relatively equalitarian distribution of resources among the veteran and the new population.	Mass immigration has lowered the educational level of the population.
	The correlation between continent of origin and level of education and of income has created a severe problem. There are great differences between veterans and new immigrants and between the European-American and African-Asian immigrants.

Natural Resources

Efforts are being made to exploit the rather limited natural resources: potash, phosphates, and copper.

Limited water resources have been mobilized to provide flexible use, by linking the water resources of the north with the parched land of the south; however, the cost may have been exorbitant.

The shortage of water makes it unlikely that as much as half of the area suitable for cultivation will be cultivated in the foreseeable future.

Natural resources are very limited; thus, most industries must be based on imported fuel and raw material.

Agriculture

Land ownership is mainly public (93 per cent), and there is no basic "agrarian problem."

There is no large underdeveloped agricultural sector, marked by disguised unemployment.

Agriculture is varied, modern, and highly mechanized.

Agricultural output provides much of domestic food consumption, raw material for the food and textile industries, and Israel's major export item—citrus fruits.

A strong system of agricultural cooperatives, stressing cooperative purchases and sales, and mutual help (even communal consumption in kibbutzim) has aided efficiency and reduced risks.

In recent years, as farm surpluses have become a serious problem, new agricultural settlement has virtually ceased.

The concentration of land ownership in public hands has often made for allocation of land to farm units on noneconomic principles.

Units are small, and owing to the high cost of water, they are uncompetitive in many products.

During the Mandate, agriculture became ideologically important, and in the eyes of many policy makers, it has remained above mere economic considerations.

Agricultural production is subsidized in order to insure high farm income; the result has been to distort relative prices of inputs and outputs, with a consequent misallocation of resources.

(continued)

Positive Factors	Negative Factors
Industry	
Since 1956 industry has received increased attention through budgetary and other incentives.	Industrial expansion is very much the result of virtually complete protection; consequently it is difficult to ascertain how much of Israel's industry has developed along lines of present —let alone future—comparative advantage, or what dislocation will eventuate when industry has to face international competition.
Manufacturing has grown faster than the rest of the economy in terms of employment, output, and exports.	
Increasing efforts are being made to plan industrial development; in particular, industrial complexes are given priority.	Bureaucratic intervention is extensive.
In recent years, more economic consideration has been given to the evaluation of industrial projects.	Units are frequently too small to be efficient; on the other hand, when there are only a few large producers, restraint of competition is common.
Infrastructure	
Large infrastructure investments have been made in ports, railroads, roads, power, and communications.	Relatively large sums have been invested in pseudo-infrastructure investments, such as shipping and airlines, whose contributions as regards external economies are questionable.
Institutions basic to a modern market economy are by now well-developed; e.g., commercial credit institutions, a securities market, emergency and pension funds, specialized development banks.	Despite a general improvement in recent years, insufficient attention has been given to investment in human resources through education. However, the existing level is still quite high compared to most developing countries.

Climate for Private Investment

Although all the coalition governments so far have been dominated by "socialist" parties, there has been no pressure to frighten off private enterprise, at least not since the very early years.

The official attitude has been that there is room in Israel for all kinds of initiative, and that the public sector should step in where private initiative is lacking.

In recent years, government activity has been shifting toward intervention largely through the price mechanism rather than through direct administrative controls.

The beneficial effects of private foreign investment as a source of funds, know-how, and initiative are appreciated; objections to foreign investment have not been a major political consideration at all during the last decade.

Laws for the encouragement of foreign investment have been enacted, and administrative efforts to attract such investments have been highly successful since 1960.

There is still little evidence of official awareness that competitive forces operating through the market mechanism are a more efficient means of allocating resources than bureaucratic decision.

Because of the fervent desire to attract foreign investment, not enough attention has been given to selectivity.

Capital inflow from foreign investment has been an important source of inflationary pressure in recent years; some of this "investment" is undoubtedly merely a means used by local firms to evade domestic credit restrictions.

(continued)

Positive Factors	Negative Factors
Balance of Payments	
Exports have expanded rapidly.	No trend toward elimination of the import surplus is as yet evident.
Exports are becoming more diversified, with the traditional exports of citrus and diamonds now supplemented by clothing, plywood, foodstuffs, transportation, tourism, and numerous other items.	Gross payment of interest has risen to some 13 per cent of gross exports in 1964.
Imports have shifted from finished goods to raw materials and semi-finished goods.	
An easier foreign exchange situation—particularly the accumulation of some $600 million in foreign exchange reserves—has made it possible to rely less on trade agreements, so that there is a more economically sound geographic distribution of foreign trade.	
Foreign Aid	
Foreign aid has provided resources which made possible a massive investment program and the provision of extensive social services to new immigrants.	Foreign aid has frequently been "tied," either as regards country of purchase or type of goods, thereby limiting somewhat the freedom to choose according to purely economic criteria.
Technical assistance and private investment have helped in the selection and implementation of investment projects.	Part of foreign aid, such as German restitutions, has exerted strong inflationary influences at the same time as it eased the foreign exchange position.
Most of the foreign assistance was in the form of unilateral transfers; the debt burden imposed was thus relatively small.	Foreign aid is expected to decline in the near future and to change in composition to more burdensome forms of financing.

3.

The Reasons for Taiwan's High Growth Rate

Shigeto Kawano

The Author

SHIGETO KAWANO is Professor of Agricultural Economics at the University of Tokyo and an Advisor to the Institute of Asian Economic Affairs. He has taught at the university since his graduation in 1936, and he holds a doctorate in agriculture from the University of Kyoto. He is a member of the Japan Association of International Economy and other agricultural and economic associations. Mr. Kawano has conducted studies in Taiwan, Southeast Asia, the United States, and Europe. He has written two books, *The Rice Economy in Formosa* and *Agricultural Problems in Japan*, as well as numerous articles on agriculture and the economic growth of underdeveloped countries.

Contents

A Remarkably High Economic Growth Rate 125

Negative and Positive Factors 130
    Negative Factors 130
    Positive Factors 133

**Effective Capital Formation Supported
by Aid from the United States** 140
    Foreign Aid and the Inflow of Foreign Capital 141
    Promotion of Domestic Capital Accumulation 142
    Efficient Disposition of Investment 144

Selective Fostering of Industry 146

Conclusion 154

Tables

1:	Average Annual Rates of Growth in Real Aggregate and Per Capita Product, 1950–59	126
2:	Selected Advanced Countries of the World: Percentage Rates of Growth of Real Aggregate and Per Capita Product in the Early Stage of Growth	126
3:	Indicators of Taiwan Economy Growth Rate	129
4:	Education of Persons Age Six and Over	129
5:	Area of Cultivated Land: Paddy Field	136
6:	Composition of Fixed Capital Formation	144
7:	Planned Allocation of Public Investment by Industry	146
8:	Import Duty, Import Substitution and Export of Selected Manufactured Commodities, 1955 and 1962	150
9:	Composition of Exports and Imports	151

A Remarkably High Economic Growth Rate

The rate of economic growth in Taiwan is not only the highest among the countries of the United Nations Economic Commission for Asia and the Far East (ECAFE) Region, with the exception of Japan, but it is also extremely high when compared with the growth rates of the countries of western Europe and America. In the period 1950-1959, according to the United Nations' *Economic Survey of Asia and the Far East, 1961,* Taiwan's growth rate stands highest at 7.9 per cent, surpassing even the 7.5 per cent of Western Germany.[1] This rate of growth is considered to be higher than the rates of growth attained by the "developed countries" at earlier stages of economic growth. According to a study by S. Kuznets[2] these rates were much lower than the growth rate of Taiwan, practically all countries being in the range of from 2.5 per cent to 4 per cent.

At 4.2 per cent, Taiwan's yearly rate of growth of national product per capita is the highest in the ECAFE Region. On the other hand, the rate of population increase is also the highest in the region. This means that the total gross national product (GNP), national product per capita, and rate of population increase are the highest in the ECAFE region. Further, the rate of

---

1. See Table 1.
2. Simon S. Kuznets, "Population, Income and Capital" in *Economic Progress* (Louvain, 1955), pp. 43-44, quoted in Economic Commission for Asia and the Far East, *Economic Survey of Asia and the Far East, 1961* (New York: United Nations, 1962), and represented here in Table 2.

126 THE REASONS FOR TAIWAN'S HIGH GROWTH RATE

Table 1: Average Annual Rates of Growth in Real Aggregate and Per Capita Product, 1950–1959

	Growth Rate Per Cent Per Annum	
	Aggregate Product (%)	Per Capita Product (%)
Country		
China: Taiwan	7.9	4.2
Philippines	6.0	2.7
Burma	5.1	3.9
Korea, South	5.0	2.1
Thailand	5.0	1.9
Cambodia	4.0	1.3
Ceylon	3.9	1.4
Indonesia	3.6	1.6
India	3.1	1.1
Pakistan	2.6	0.4
Japan	9.1	7.9
Germany (Federal Republic)	7.5	...

Source: Economic Commission for Asia and the Far East, *Economic Survey of Asia and the Far East: 1961* (New York: United Nations, 1962), pp. 11-12.

Table 2: Selected Advanced Countries of the World: Percentage Rates of Growth of Real Aggregate and Per Capita Product in the Early Stage of Growth

Country and Period	Annual Rate of Growth of Aggregate Product (%)	Annual Rate of Growth of Per Capita Product (%)
Japan, 1878-1907	4.6	3.4
United States, 1869-1908	4.3	2.2
Canada, 1870-1910	3.8	2.3
Germany, 1860-1899	3.8	2.8
Italy, 1861-1900	3.3	2.6
Denmark, 1870-1909	3.1	2.0
Australia, 1901-1930	3.0	1.2
Switzerland, 1890-1929	2.6	1.9
United Kingdom, 1860-1899	2.6	1.5
Sweden, 1861-1890	2.5	1.8
France, 1840-1899	1.7	1.5

Source: Economic Commission for Asia and the Far East, *Economic Survey of Asia and the Far East: 1961* (New York: United Nations, 1962), p. 12.

4.2 per cent is much higher than those of the developed countries at the stages referred to above. The highest of these, that of Japan, was no more than 3.4 per cent and almost all the rest were between 2 per cent and 1 per cent.

It is generally believed that the reason for the high growth rates of the developing countries is that, as "late starters," these countries were able to make use of modern technology in a more profitable manner, that they were able to use "ready made" forms of technology which the developed countries had developed at the expense of much time and cost through a process of trial and error. It need hardly be said that technology cannot be simply transplanted from one place to another as "knowledge," but it will scarcely be disputed that, provided certain conditions are fulfilled, it is probable that modern technology will be adopted in a rapid and profitable manner by the countries which are later recipients of the tradition. In cases where this occurs one may suppose that the required conditions have been fulfilled.

At the same time, however, these countries have markedly high rates of population growth. This is a factor operating in the direction of lowering the growth rate of per capita incomes. The rates of population increase in the developed countries during the earlier stages of economic growth were almost all less than 1.5 per cent, exceptions being the United States (2.1 per cent) and Australia (1.8 per cent), but in almost all cases the rates of population growth in the late developing countries are over 2.0 per cent, the average being up at 2.5 per cent.

This increase in population is almost entirely due to "natural increase," the result of a sudden lowering of the death rate by the introduction of modern medicine and therapeutics and the improvement of conditions of hygiene. This may be expressed the other way round by saying that in spite of the decline in the death rate there has been no decline in the birth rate. Early marriage, the absence of birth-control or resistance to its introduction, and other customs or patterns of living which maintain a high birth rate have survived and are not easily subject to change. The gap between the two has produced the large "natural increase."

As a general rule, this phenomenon occurs in all cases in

which a process of industrialization is carried out. It has been experienced by the countries of western Europe. The special characteristic of the case of the late developing countries, however, is that the decline in death rates has been so sudden and widespread that the difference between the birth rates and death rates—the "natural increase" rates—have been markedly high. Consequently, the results of economic growth have been largely absorbed by population increase, producing increases in per capita incomes which are scarcely worth having. Further, by this mechanism the difference between the per capita incomes of the developed countries and the developing countries has tended to grow greater and greater.

Nevertheless, among the developing countries Taiwan has the highest rate of population increase among the countries of the Asian region, while, as I have noted, the growth rate of its national product is particularly high, and the growth rate of its per capita income also the highest. What were the socio-economic factors which made this possible?

In 1945 Taiwan emerged as an independent country after fifty years of Japanese rule. The years following its independence were, of course, accompanied by considerable social and economic disruption. It was only after 1953, when the first Four-Year Plan for economic construction began, that the economy embarked on steady development. Four such plans for economic construction have been carried out since then. Their results may be seen in the annual rates of growth since 1953.[3] Over the period 1953–65 the average annual rate of growth of the real national income has been 7.8 per cent, that of the per capita national income 4.4 per cent, that of agricultural production 6.1 per cent and that of industrial production 12.9 per cent. Considered as percentages of the figures of 1952, the 1965 figures for real national income stand at 263.6, those for per capita income at 173.2, those for agricultural production at 214.7, and those for industrial production at 486.0. From these figures one can discern a rapid progress in industrialization.

What is more, the growth rates of the 1960's are higher

---

3. See Table 3.

Table 3: Indicators of Taiwan Economy Growth Rate

Year	Population (%)	Real National Income (%)	Per Capita Income (%)	Agricultural Production (%)	Industrial Production (%)
1953	3.8	15.1	11.3	14.2	24.1
1954	3.7	4.0	0.4	2.0	7.2
1955	3.8	6.2	2.1	2.4	11.1
1956	3.4	5.4	2.1	6.5	5.1
1957	3.2	6.7	3.5	10.5	13.6
1958	3.6	5.6	2.2	8.2	7.6
1959	3.9	6.9	3.6	2.2	13.1
1960	3.5	7.5	4.2	−0.5	13.8
1961	3.3	8.0	4.7	10.6	10.5
1962	3.3	6.2	3.1	1.3	12.8
1963	3.2	6.5	3.4	3.6	10.1
1964	3.1	16.6	13.2	10.3	25.8
1965	3.0	6.4	3.3	8.7	15.0
1953–65 average	3.4	7.8	4.4	6.1	12.9

Source: *Taiwan Statistical Data Book*, 1966, p. 2.

Table 4: Education of Persons Age Six and Over
(per cent)

Year	Total	Higher Education	Secondary Education	Primary Education	Others	Illiterate
1952	100	1.4	8.8	43.5	4.2	42.1
1953	100	1.4	9.0	44.1	4.0	41.5
1954	100	1.6	9.3	45.5	3.9	39.7
1955	100	1.7	9.6	46.9	3.9	37.9
1956	100	1.7	9.6	47.7	3.9	37.1
1957	100	1.7	10.8	51.0	4.2	32.3
1958	100	1.8	11.2	51.4	4.7	30.9
1959	100	1.8	11.7	53.3	4.3	28.9
1960	100	1.9	12.4	54.1	4.5	27.1
1961	100	1.9	13.0	55.0	4.2	25.9
1962	100	2.0	13.7	55.3	4.2	24.8
1963	100	2.2	14.5	55.5	4.2	23.6
1964	100	2.3	15.3	56.0	4.0	22.4
1965	100	2.3	15.2	55.4	4.0	23.1

Source: *Taiwan Statistical Data Book*, 1966, p. 6.

than those of the 1950's. Further, the results of the increase in per capita incomes have revealed themselves in such outwardly visible changes as increased attendance at institutions of education at all levels, from primary school through middle school and from high school to university, and in a decline in the illiteracy rate. The number of illiterate persons aged six years or over stood at 42.1 per cent in 1952, but had declined to 23.1 per cent by 1965, while the number of persons with records of attendance at high schools or universities increased during the same period from 1.4 per cent to 2.3 per cent. Again, the numbers of medical personnel (including physicians, dentists, nurses, and midwives) and of medical institutions (including general hospitals, health centers, and mobile medical units) were all roughly doubled in the period 1952-65. Not only did individual levels of consumption rise, but social overhead capital was also greatly expanded. By what means was this high rate of economic growth brought about?

Negative and Positive Factors

Among the basic factors governing the economic growth of Taiwan may be cited negative factors and positive factors.

Negative Factors

The first negative factor was the sudden increase in population resulting from the great inflow of population when the Chiang Kai-shek regime moved into the island in 1949, supervening on the lowered economic levels of the World War II and postwar periods. Taiwan was restored to China in 1945, but it is said that under the conditions of social and economic unrest which characterized the postwar period, supervening on the economic difficulties of wartime, production declined to almost less than 50 per cent of the level reached under Japanese rule. Compared with the highest production figures attained under Japanese rule the 1945 figures for the production of rice stood at 45 per cent and for coal, sugar, and cement at less than 30 per cent, a spectacular fall in production.

The establishment of a Communist regime on the Chinese mainland also resulted in a great influx of population from the continent. As a consequence, the 1946 population of 6,090,000 was increased to 12,628,000 (exclusive of military personnel) by 1965. It is estimated that during this period there was a population influx from the continent of between 2,000,000 and 2,500,000. This means that there was a sudden population increase amounting to roughly one-third of the indigenous population in the space of a few years after the war. If other conditions remained unchanged, this must have been a factor producing a decline in marginal productivity, and, as a result, a decline of per capita income. If to this is added the disruption of the social and economic order occasioned by the influx of population, this factor becomes all the more destructive. Of course not all the population which came in from the continent was entirely without capital or property. There was an influx of capital in the textile business and in other parts of the economy. Nevertheless, the immediate effect was a lowering of income per person as a whole. This resulted in an unavoidable decline of consumption to below customary levels. At the same time, since consumer demand was steady in the short term, a high propensity to consume was continually operative as a factor in keeping down the rate of capital accumulation.

The second factor was the high level of the rate of natural increase of population, more than 3 per cent. The effects of this factor, continuously in operation from day to day, produced only imperceptible differences, and their economic significance was the same as in the case of the first factor. When other conditions, such as available capital, technological conditions, etc., remain the same, an increase in population is a factor producing a decline in marginal productivity and consequently in average income levels. Again, the numbers of the nonproductive age groups (under 15 and over 60) expressed as a percentage of the productive age groups (ages 15 to 59) rose markedly from 86.8 per cent in 1952 to 99.1 per cent in 1965. This meant an increase in the burden of maintenance per capita, and, assuming that the productive capacity per capita in the productive age-groups remained the same, it also meant that there was a similar increase in the proportion of per capita incomes directed to consumption.

By means of this increase in the proportion of the national income devoted to consumption and the decline in the proportion devoted to capital accumulation the conditions for a fall in the average productivity can be provided. In fact, the proportion of employed persons expressed as a percentage of total population showed a marked decrease, from 36.1 per cent in 1952 to 29.7 per cent in 1965. This decline suggests most strikingly that this did occur. Assuming that no interference with propensities to consume took place, this would be a factor making for a gradual increase in the proportion of the national income consumed.

The third factor was the burden of military expenditure. Because of the absence of source material, I am unable to make clear the details of government finance in Taiwan. It is believed that 80 per cent of the revenues of the central government, or about 50 per cent of the total government budget covering the central and provincial administrations, is devoted to defense expenditure. In the light of the fact that government expenditure is considered to constitute 21 per cent of gross national product (1956-61), this would seem to constitute about 10 per cent. It need hardly be said that this represents a corresponding necessary reduction of levels of consumption or of productive investment. Every country has its burden of military expenditure, and it is difficult to deny that military expenditure is a positive factor favoring economic growth through the political stability which it produces. Nevertheless, when the question is considered from the point of view of the distribution of a given quantity of income, it cannot be denied that military spending results in a corresponding reduction in productive investment.

Fourth, in a certain sense the population-mass of 12,000,000 persons is too small. This may appear to be contradictory to our statements concerning the first and second factors, but this is not necessarily the case. The latest advances in industrial technology have rendered the advantages of a large-scale economy overwhelmingly profitable; but large-scale economy is brought into being by the possession of a large domestic market, in which population is one important factor. As forms of production are raised to higher levels, the minimum scale of operation required in production is enlarged, and the adoption of these kinds of industry is difficult for small countries because of the smallness of the domestic market and the dearth of labor and other resources.

This is clear from the fact that while all countries have agricultural industry in which the economy of scale is relatively small, large-scale enterprises—heavy industries such as steel production, shipbuilding, and automobile manufacture—which require large scale production to achieve a certain degree of profit are restricted to the countries with a sizable domestic market. Furthermore, the reasons for the existence of the European Economic Community (EEC) and other movements for the establishment of economic integration lie in the desire to gain the advantages of a large-scale economy which would result from such arrangements. From this point of view one must conclude that Taiwan is a small country as regards population and domestic market. Consequently one must conclude that, to this extent, there are restrictions on the profitability of large-scale economy and the adoption of large-scale and heavy industries. Insofar as this is so there are restrictions on total economic growth. This means that the types of industry which can be adopted rationally and efficiently are subjected to restrictions and limitations by the size of the national economy.

Positive Factors

In contrast to the above, the following positive factors may be cited. The first of these is Taiwan's succession to the social and economic inheritance of the period of Japanese rule. This inheritance covers a large number of aspects.

a) The first of these is the high degree of investment in the "human factor." By origin the people of Taiwan are descendants of colonists from the Chinese continent who, filled with the spirit of adventure and positive aspirations, came to the island to bring virgin land under cultivation. They are a people devoted to hard work and close application. They are racially homogeneous, and within their homogeneity there are no castes. The restriction or prescription of economic activities by religion is not found among them, a point on which they differ from some other developing countries. In language there are differences, for instance between the Fukkien and Canton Dialect speakers, but the nation is bound together by a common script. Economic motivation provides ample stimulus to mobility of the human factor between industries, occupations and regions, and this has been the guiding force. A modern educational system has been gradually, and without compulsion, introduced into this milieu. The result has been a lowering of the illiteracy rate, at least in comparison with other Asian countries. For example, in 1946 the illiteracy rate among persons over six years of age was approximately 55 per cent, which is a good deal lower than the rates in India (81 per cent of persons over 15 years of age) and Indonesia (65 per cent according to the United Nation's *Statistical Yearbook, 1957*). It was believed that, to the extent that this was so, it would bring about a condition favorable to the development of the country as a whole. This is because the raising of levels of technology and the transmission of technical knowledge can be carried out all the more effectively and speedily if the people can read and write.

The year-by-year decline in the illiteracy rate bore testimony to the fact that the people of Taiwan had already recognized the economic effectiveness of education by their own daily experience. A tendency to spontaneous investment in education was deeply rooted among them. For this reason the burden of investment and political efforts required in education in Taiwan were light in comparison with those cases in which the government must tenaciously propagandize the need for education and for the spread of education itself. It must also be said that the efficiency of Taiwan's educational system was high. The conditions are thus quite different from those reported from countries where there has been little or no national interest in or desire for educational progress.

b) This rise in Taiwan's levels of education produced in corresponding measure a labor force possessed of certain technical skills—supervisory workers, office workers, and skilled workers—and left behind, after the Japanese withdrawal, a body of professional personnel capable of running modern administrative organizations and business enterprises. It need hardly be said that during the period of Japanese rule the top ranks of staff and workers in government offices, business companies, and factories were mostly Japanese. But below them, in addition to the general workers, there were native clerks, engineers, etc., ready to take their places with comparative ease and rapidity.

By 1939 Taiwan's industrial production had exceeded its agricultural production in value, and this tendency was becoming stronger in 1945. In that year there were approximately 120,000 private enterprises run by Taiwan nationals in industries other than agriculture and forestry. They employed 130,000 persons. The incorporated enterprises with a capital of more than Y 100,000 (about $150,000 at present values) were mostly run by Japanese, but, with the inclusion of some run by Taiwan nationals, these amounted to 2,700, and employed 174,000 persons.[4] It may easily be inferred that these constituted the central labor force for later economic development of Taiwan.

Among those who came into the island from the continent after the war there were many educated people who had enjoyed high standards of living in the European style in Shanghai, Hongkong, and elsewhere. Both within and outside the government service they took part in drawing up and implementing economic policies, and thereby helped promote Taiwan's recent economic growth. A very high proportion of the civil servants in the Taiwan Provincial, Hsien, and Chen Administrations consists of "persons from outside the Province" (immigrants from the continent). In 1950 this proportion was estimated to have been 35 per cent, and in 1956, 45 per cent.[5] One must take into con-

---

4. T. Sasamoto, ed. *The Industrial Structure of Taiwan* (in Japanese), 1964, pp. 224–227.
5. Taiwan State, *Statistical Abstract,* 1960, p. 36.

sideration the fact that these people would tend to choose government positions. The situation in Taiwan, however, is greatly different from the majority of the developing countries in which training of officials, industrialists, and technicians to run the modern administrative apparatus and business enterprises must be undertaken from the beginning.

c) A fair degree of modern technology had been introduced into all branches of industry. Certain forms of technology suitable to the natural conditions of Taiwan also were invented and applied. The technological conditions for economic development were fairly well provided. It was the sugar manufacturing industry which played the role of the pioneer in the industrialization of Taiwan. Modern technology was introduced into this industry at an early period, and when work began on other industries, such as electric power supply, cement, and chemical fertilizer, the forms of technology which had been applied in the developed countries were transplanted unchanged into Taiwan. These technological introductions were such as could be expected to be comparatively easily transplantable, provided that modern machinery was introduced and that the operational personnel were educated up to the required levels of skill, since they were unaffected by any restrictions imposed by the conditions of the natural environment. As I have noted, the conditions of skill in the labor force were provided.

In the case of transplanting agricultural technology, however, it was not easy to produce the plant varieties that were required by the natural environment. An improved variety of sugar

Table 5: Area of Cultivated Land: Paddy Field
(unit: 1000 Ha)

Year	Grand Total	Total	Double-cropping Field	Single-Cropping Field	Upland Field
1940	860.456	529.611	324.209	205.412	330.835
1952	876.1	533.6	325.1	208.5	342.5
1955	873.0	532.7	332.7	200.0	340.3
1960	869.2	525.6	329.1	196.5	343.6
1963	872.2	528.7	329.3	199.4	343.5
1965	889.6	536.8	337.5	199.3	352.8

Source: *Taiwan Statistical Data Book*, 1966, p. 19.

cane suited to large applications of fertilizers was imported from Java during the period of Japanese rule. This variety was further improved and good results were produced in a comparatively short time. The native rice, however, was scarcely capable of absorbing fertilizers effectively. The Japanese varieties which could absorb fertilizers effectively were unsuitable under the natural conditions of Taiwan. The Japanese varieties made growth in the leaves and the stalks but did not produce a high yield of grain. Taiwan growers then proceeded to improve the native varieties and adapt the Japanese varieties to the natural conditions of Taiwan, although it was 25 years before success was attained. It was about 1925 that the fruits of the government experimental stations established in the first decade of the century were gathered for the first time.[6] Consequently, as has already been mentioned, a great fall in rice production took place at the end of the World War II, principally because of a lack of fertilizers, but this was of such a nature that it could be expected to be easily restorable, provided that the supply of fertilizers were restored.

A similar situation prevailed in the case of sugar. In other crops, such as pineapple, the conditions were already provided for cultivation with heavy fertilizer applications. Again, since the experimental and research stations required for the improvement of varieties and the organization required for agricultural extension had been built up, one may assume that the technological preconditions for agricultural development in general had been completed. On this point, too, Taiwan differs from the majority of the developing countries, where agriculture without fertilizers is predominant, and plant varieties are adapted to this environmental condition. Yields cannot be raised simply by making available increased supplies of fertilizers. Not only do the stalks of the plants alone flourish while no increase takes place in the grain, but there are many instances in which the contrary occurs and a decline in yields takes place.

Consequently, in these circumstances, work must begin from the invention of new plant varieties and new techniques. In

---

6. S. Kawano, *Rice Economy in Taiwan,* (in Japanese), 1941.

order to do this it is necessary to go the round-about route of starting from the training of research workers and the institution of new organizations. Since the restoration, technicians have been sent out from the United States, the countries of western Europe, and Japan for the purposes of raising levels of technology. The dispatch of trainees to these countries, together with other schemes, is being carried on. This presupposes the completion of some basic conditions such as those which have been mentioned above.

d) The fourth factor is the filling out of "social overhead capital." This commences with water control (comprising flood control, irrigation, drainage, etc.) and the fitting out of the transport and communications systems (roads, railways, etc.). Water control, in particular, was the object of efforts in Taiwan from a comparatively early period. The topography is mountainous and the terrain liable to flooding in the typhoon season, while the distinct rainy and dry seasons make it difficult to maintain an even and stable supply of water from natural sources throughout the year. The main emphasis was placed on turning unirrigated agricultural land into irrigated rice fields to be used for producing two crops of rice per year whenever possible. After 1918, when Japan experienced rice riots as a result of food shortages, the government bent its efforts to the reclamation of land for use as rice fields and the expansion of irrigation facilities. There has been practically no substantial change in the total cultivated area or the area devoted to irrigated rice in Taiwan in the last 25 years. As far as investment in agricultural water-control is concerned, the facilities provided in the period of Japanese rule still constitute the major basis of the rice industry.

Efforts were made to increase agricultural production—as will be shown later—by using the land intensively and by introducing diversification into production. By this means it has become possible to maintain a large number of peasant household (60 per cent more than prewar, taking the period 1940–65). This fact means that to this extent there had been no small saving in investment in agricultural water control. One may therefore take this as meaning that to this extent the positive conditions for agricultural production were provided.

As regards transport and communications, it is true that since 1953 there has been an absolute increase in the number and capacity of railway rolling stock, in the mileage of highways, and in the numbers of city telephones, but the rates of increase have been very modest. The mileages of railway track and highways, in particular, have been more or less static and have been altogether unable to compensate for population increase. As a result, the existing facilities, like the agricultural land, are being used more intensively, and this is profitable in that it makes possible saving in new large-scale and long-term investment in this sector of the economy. In transport there has been a marked increase in motor vehicles, but this case differs from road construction in that the increase takes place one vehicle at a time. Provided that roads are already in existence no large-scale or lump-sum investment is necessarily required in this sector of economy. If one may judge by the results, it has been possible to "make do" with investments in new transport and communications facilities which are small in comparison with those made in other countries. The question of the over-intensive use of roads must be considered, but at the least it seems apparent that past investments can be utilized to a fair degree. This is, to some extent, a positive factor for economic growth.

e) Fifth, the fact that Taiwan is a small insular country makes it easy to carry out effectively political measures designed to produce social stability and to put economic plans into operation. Legislation to control political unrest under severe penalties has, of course, been enacted. The use of stern measures to suppress the disruption of production by industrial disputes emphasize the need for greater cooperation between labor and employers. Penalties for infringements of food-control and anti-usury laws are also enforced. Steps have been taken both institutionally and from the point of view of personnel, to enforce controls with thoroughness. These measures have helped to carry out these national economic plans within their allotted time schedules.

Further, it has been necessary to enforce a certain degree of political regulation of the distribution of incomes, the distribution of investments, and the flow of material goods and services. This is aimed at giving maximum encouragement to capital accumulation from the lower-income levels and to investments made at selected points in accordance with plans. The conditions for the effective implementation of such economic plans are provided by these political measures. It is a characteristic that, of the four Four-Year Plans which have been carried out in Taiwan, the discrepancies between plans and performance are very small, at least in the sphere of investment. I am inclined to believe that, if the indications provided by the statistical source material are not erroneous, one of the reasons for the success of these plans is to be found in this factor.

In the above I have analyzed the positive and negative factors governing economic growth in Taiwan, factors which may be described as the basic conditions under which economic growth takes place. The next problem is what kind of political measures were actually taken in order to produce a high rate of economic growth on the foundations of these basic conditions.

Effective Capital Formation Supported by Aid from the United States

In theory a high rate of economic growth is brought about by no other means than an efficient utilization of limited resources. There are, however, two aspects of this question. The first is the supply of capital, and the second is its investment. It is desirable that as large a sum of capital as possible should be procured, and that investment should be carried out with maximum efficiency.

In regard to the supply of capital there are two aspects— foreign aid and the inflow of foreign capital on the one hand, and saving out of domestic product on the other.

Foreign Aid and the Inflow of Foreign Capital

In terms of aid per head of population in the period 1950–59, Taiwan is one of the Asian countries which receive the largest amounts of foreign aid. Foreign aid amounted to an annual average of $8.56 per head of population, following Laos, South Vietnam, and Korea.[7] The aiding country, it need hardly be said, was the United States of America, and the amount of aid granted in the years 1951–61 alone is said to have reached a total of $1,155,000,000.

This aid was more or less sufficient to cover deficits in the international balance of payments in each year. During the same period, deficits amounted to approximately 60 per cent of the value of exports. Since exports are estimated to have been approximately 9 per cent of gross national product, one may suppose that aid amounted to approximately 5 per cent of gross national product.

The burden of Taiwan's military expenditures, amounting to 10 per cent of gross national product, was reduced to almost one-half by foreign aid. A rate of military expenditure amounting to 5 per cent of gross national product cannot be described as low, but one must recognize the fact that the problem of the burden of military expenditure, to which I referred above, was at least partially mitigated in this way.

Foreign aid not only constituted a simple addition to the purchasing power of this country but it also made possible the direct purchase from foreign countries of capital goods and raw materials necessary for economic development. This is another important significance of foreign aid for economic development.

As regards foreign capital, in general a policy was adopted of giving positive encouragement to shareholding participation in foreign investment on the part of all the import-substitute industries and export industries, with the exception of the sugar industry and the petroleum industry. In 1954 steps were taken to promote such investment with the help of legal enactments relating to investment by foreigners. In particular, since the

---

7. *Economic Survey of Asia and the Far East: 1961, op. cit.,* p. 49.

issue of the regulations governing investment by Chinese abroad in 1955, steps have been taken to promote the inflow of their capital by preferential treatment in the fields of taxation, the acquisition of building sites, etc.

Because of this, the proportion of foreign nongovernment investment in the total value of imports of goods and services is appreciably higher than in the other Asian countries. In the period 1957-62 it reached an annual average of 10.2 per cent, coming second to the Philippines with 12.5 per cent.[8] The inflow of private capital, of course, presupposes as a necessary condition that present profitability is high or has some prospect of being high in the future. If we compare Taiwan with certain other countries in which a restrictive and prohibitive attitude is adopted to foreign investment, we may consider that Taiwan's policies themselves, which have been aimed at facilitating the acceptance of investment, have had a great effect.

The Promotion of Domestic Capital Accumulation

Included in saving out of national product are private voluntary saving and compulsory or semi-compulsory saving brought about through financial policies. It need not be said that it is difficult to expect a high rate of voluntary saving under circumstances such as those which have been described above, in which a sudden inflow of population has supervened on a fall in production. In Taiwan this situation was dealt with by means of saving effected through government financial measures, particularly by indirect taxation. Government expenditures, as I have noted, amounted to 21 per cent of gross national product, while normal government revenues amounted to 16 per cent of gross national product, the difference being made up by foreign aid and the issuance of government bonds. Since the sale of government bonds had the effect of causing a rise in prices, this measure was very much in the nature of a form of indirect taxation. Seventeen per cent of normal government revenue was

---

8. Economic Commission for Asia and the Far East, *Economic Survey of Asia and the Far East: 1963,* (New York: United Nations, 1964), p. 12.

derived from tobacco and wine monopolies, 22 per cent from income from public enterprises and public property, and the remaining 61 per cent from taxation. Of the income from taxation, about two-thirds was derived from indirect taxes, such as customs duties and commodity taxes.[9] It need hardly be said that taxes on the tobacco and wine monopolies are indirect taxes on the consuming public. In the case of the public enterprise electric companies, sugar companies, fertilizer companies, etc., the income from these companies also partakes of the nature of taxes on the public, or indirect taxation in no small degree, in consequence of the monopolistic character of these undertakings. In regard to this system I must note that the monopolies were continued unchanged from the period of Japanese rule. The public enterprise companies were built up on the foundations of powerful enterprises established in the period of Japanese rule which were continued. With these government financial arrangements as the center, positive investment in government organs and public enterprises was pushed forward, and, as an integral part of this, levels of investment as a whole were raised.

Gross capital formation including increase in stocks as a percentage of gross national product has been rising from year to year, and, in particular, since 1961 it has been well up to 22 per cent.[10] Fixed capital formation has increased at the same time, but about half of it is occupied by government and public enterprise. In this process part of these enterprises was sold off to private enterprise and so the weight of public enterprise in fixed capital formation declined, but government investment still amounted to 15 per cent. It is true that one-third of the total sum actually invested was covered by aid from the United States. I have reason to believe that, without the financial policies described above, the direction of aid funds into investment would itself have been no easily accomplished task. I say this because, if financial income had proved insufficient at any time, there would have been every possibility of the greater part of foreign

---

9. All figures for 1956–61. *Taiwan Statistical Data Book*, 1964, pp. 88–89.
10. See Table 6.

Table 6: Composition of Fixed Capital Formation

Year	Gross Capital Formation in Gross National Product (%)	Government (%)	Public Enterprises (%)	Private and Household (%)
1952	18.3	18.8	26.4	54.8
1953	16.6	14.9	30.0	55.1
1954	16.9	18.4	23.2	58.4
1955	15.3	15.2	34.5	50.4
1956	15.0	16.2	39.4	44.4
1957	16.4	18.7	39.9	41.4
1958	18.2	19.9	40.4	39.7
1959	19.9	23.0	33.0	44.0
1960	21.7	21.0	27.7	51.3
1961	22.0	19.7	31.4	48.9
1962	21.0	20.3	28.2	51.5
1963	17.4	13.6	32.2	54.2
1964	18.8	15.3	24.9	59.8

Source: *Taiwan Statistical Data Book*, 1966, pp. 15-16.

aid being consumed in simple administrative expenses or in raising the consumption level of the people by lowering prices.

International comparisions with the fixed capital formation of Taiwan show that on the average for the years 1957-59 the rate of gross capital formation stood at 14.7 per cent, a figure not as high as those for Burma (19.2 per cent), India (17.4 per cent), or Thailand (15.2 per cent), but fairly high in comparison with the figures for other Asia countries.[11] However, in 1957 the domestic net saving rate was 5 per cent of net national product, and since this figure had been raised to 9 per cent by 1961 one must conclude that considerable policy efforts have been made in capital formation.[12]

Efficient Disposition of Investment

However, it is the efficient disposition of these investments which sustains the high rate of economic growth in Taiwan. This appears econometrically in the fact that the incre-

---

11. *Economic Survey of Asia and the Far East: 1961, op. cit.,* p. 23.
12. *Economic Survey of Asia and the Far East: 1963, op. cit.,* p. 25.

mental capital output ratio for Taiwan for the average of the years 1950-59 given by the ECAFE annual reports stands at the remarkably low figure of 1.7. The corresponding figures for the three countries mentioned above, Burma, India, and Thailand, are 3.4, 4.8, and 2.6 respectively. While these figures indicate that the rate of economic growth in these countries has been restricted in proportion to their magnitude, nevertheless the marginal rate of efficiency of investment is much higher in the case of Taiwan. The figure for Taiwan is the smallest in the Asian region, with the exception of the 1.2 figure for the Philippines. This indicates a high net rate.[13]

Two other conditions should also be considered. The first is that, because of circumstances which I have described above, there has not been so great a need for investment in the sectors of the economy requiring large-scale or long-term investment, such as transport, telecommunications, or education. Again, since there has been a fair amount of basic investment in agriculture, it has been possible to carry out concentrated investment in developing the mining, manufacturing, and energy industries. Another condition is probably the fact that in the development of these latter industries comparatively efficient management was employed in choosing industrial priorities and on the operation side.

As to the first of these conditions one must look at the figures presented in Table 7. These are planned figures, but in the distribution of public investment they show, in the case of Taiwan, that investment in transport and telecommunication is appreciably low—at 20 per cent. There is little investment in agriculture. On the other hand, investment in mining, manufacturing, and electricity is overwhelmingly large. As need hardly be said, this can be taken to indicate a belief that, while investment in the former two had already reached a fair level, there was still room for further expansion of mining, manufacturing, and agricultural production. In comparison with other countries the economy of Taiwan seems to have operated under more favorable conditions in relation to these external econo-

---

13. *Economic Survey of Asia and the Far East: 1961*, *op. cit.*, p. 24.

Table 7: Planned Allocation of Public Investment by Industry

Country	Period of Planning	Agriculture	Industry and Mining	Electricity	Transportation, communication	Total
China: Taiwan	1957-60	23	—57—		20	100
India	1956-60	28	24	11	37	100
Burma	1956-59	27	28	17	28	100
Philippines	1960-62	31	24	17	28	100
Pakistan	1955-59	41	17	17	25	100
Thailand	1961-66	42	8	3	47	100

Source: United Nations Economic Commission for Asia and the Far East, *A Decade of Development Planning and Implementation in the ECAFE Region*, Conference of Asian Economic Planners, 1st Session, 1961.

mies and was able to economize in investment in these sectors. It also need hardly be said that this might be a factor raising the marginal efficiency of investment. In fact, water supplies to farm land were stabilized. Wherever possible, unirrigated land was made into irrigated land. The utilization of land already used for rice was intensified, so that two crops of rice could be produced in each year. All that was lacking was an ample supply of fertilizers and materials which would make possible the fullest use of the farm land. Rice and sugar production was such that, if only the proper conditions had been provided, a restoration of production would have been accomplished with comparative ease. Carrying on from this, a positive increase in production would also have been possible.

Selective Fostering of Industry

a) The first of these is the fact that basic industries, such as electricity and fertilizers, and industries newly introduced into Taiwan, such as the chemical and metallurgical industries, were first carried on as public enterprises and operated with the help of government investment. When some of these industries became "going concerns" they were transferred to private enterprise. In the basic industries this made possible large-scale selective investment which would have been difficult for private enterprise to undertake. Its effects on the economy as a whole made possible the development of related industries.

In the case of the newly introduced industries, the inception risks were taken by public enterprise. As soon as there was some prospect of the industry standing on its own feet it was sold off to private enterprise. In 1960 there were 77 public enterprises.

The ratio between the values of production in public and private enterprise was 41 to 59, between numbers of employees 32 to 68, between the totals of funds employed 66 to 34, and between totals of funds employed per enterprise 16 to 1. It is clear that public enterprises were overwhelmingly concentrated among the large enterprises and that privately operated enterprises were small-scale businesses. But, from the fact that in 1952 the ratio between the values of production in the two types of enterprise was 60 to 40, we may deduce that there has been a gradual transfer to private enterprise.

The important publicly operated enterprises were in electricity, fertilizers, and sugar. These industries have been the objects of important selective investment throughout the period since the first four-year economic construction plan. At first, the electricity industry produced mainly hydro-electric power, but after 1962 development was centered on caloric power generation. Generating capacity increased 3 times between 1952 and 1962, and the power available per head of population is higher than in any other country in Asia, with the exception of Japan. Electricity charges are low in the international scale, and it is said that 81 per cent of this electricity (1961) is fed to industrial consumption in mining and manufacturing industry, not for domestic consumption.[14] Since this makes possible the utilization of cheap motive power this helps

---

14. *Taiwan Statistical Data Book*, 1964, p. 50.

raise the general productivity of those industries that are centered on mining and manufacturing. It has had a particularly profitable effect on those industries which use motive power on a large scale in production. The chemical fertilizer industry showed a spectacular increase in production because this situation had made possible a lowering of costs and because factories near places of consumption were able, because of transport considerations, to survive even when costs were comparatively high. By 1962 this industry was able to supply 50 per cent of domestic consumption. Nevertheless, I must note that, in the development of this fertilizer industry, a great deal of new plant was laid down, principally with the help of the aid from the United States during the period up to 1952 when the installations destroyed during the war were being restored. At any rate, this increased supply of fertilizers produced the restoration and increase of yields per unit area over the whole range of agricultural production. Rice and sugar cane were the chief crops, and they brought about, as I have noted above, an increase in the productivity of agriculture as well as a diversification of agricultural production itself.

In the case of the sugar industry, investment centered on the restoration, renovation, etc., of sugar refineries, machinery, and installations. When added to the restoration of levels of production of the raw material (sugar cane), this brought about an increase in the productivity of the sugar industry as a whole. Furthermore, rice and sugar production were able to cover the increased demand caused by the sudden increase in population and to leave a surplus for export. No special difficulties were discovered in exporting these articles, at least as far as their quality was concerned. This was because these articles had been exported to Japan before the war and it was comparatively easy to restore their quality. Further, the partial satisfaction of domestic demand for chemical fertilizers out of domestic production made possible a corresponding saving in the value of imports and lightened the burden in the international balance of payments.

Production in the cement industry was also at first carried on by public enterprises. For reasons similar to those in the fertilizer industry it was possible to compete against imports, even with high costs. Since the factories were located near the places of consumption, and had an ample supply of electric power and plentiful raw materials (to which were added protective measures in the form of a high customs tariff) domestic demand was satisfied and a surplus was left for export.

b) Second, there were among other public enterprises the aluminum-producing Lead Industries Company and the oil-refining Oil Company. Artificial fibres, textiles, alkalis, paper, steel, ship-building, and metallurgy undertakings were also carried on by publicly operated enterprises. Among these there were several undertakings which were entirely new to Taiwan and industries which expanded rapidly as a result of being carried on as public enterprises. Again, in addition to the cement industry, canning of pineapple had formerly been carried on as a publicly operated undertaking. This was transferred to private enterprise at the same time as the other undertakings. On grounds of efficient operation and the necessity of importing foreign capital the general principle has been adopted of gradually transferring these publicly operated enterprises to private enterprise. Excessive numbers of employees and low efficiency exist in some of those companies which are still operating under public management. One must recognize, however, that great contributions were made by the initial investments and risk-taking of the public form of management in developing and establishing newly introduced industries.

c) Third, steps were taken to promote domestic industries as import-substitute industries by means of a protective policy that was comprised of import controls and import tariffs placed on an enormous number of consumer goods and intermediate goods, including the products produced by these enterprises. The first of these was textiles, including cotton and synthetic fibres. In the case of the former, supplies of cheap cotton from the United States, under the disposal of surplus agricultural products, allowed self-sufficiency in this branch of production to be attained in a comparatively short time. In due course the industry went on to export part of its production. The latter product has now substituted completely for imports, and both products were originally begun as publicly operated undertakings.

For the rest, many other commodities are rapidly advancing as import substitutes.[15] It is probable that among these at least some, although only a few, still are closely protected against foreign competition by import restrictions and tariffs. These are able to survive at the expense of the consumer in a domestic market in which they enjoy a monopoly, in spite of their high costs and poor quality. Also some commodities are being exported at present which are able to survive in the export market because of preferential measures or promotive measures in the spheres of procurement of raw materials, domestic financial assistance, fiscal policy, etc. The United Nations' *Economic Survey of Asia and the Far East: 1963*, for example, had this to say:

Table 8: Import Duty, Import Substitution and Export of Selected Manufactured Commodities, 1955 and 1962

Commodity	Import Duty (%)	Production as Per Cent of Total Supply (%) 1955	1962	Export as Per Cent of Production (%) 1955	1962
Wheat	25	96	100	---	2
Gasoline	50[c]	99	100	---	11
Asphalt	10	81	95	---	55
Sulphuric Acid	30[c]	100	100	---	---
Nitric Acid	30	99	100	---	1
Caustic soda	50[c]	100	100	1	4
Printing ink	30	78	84	---	7
Nitrogeneous fertilizers (N content)	5	2	49	---	---
Plywood	35[c]	100	100	4	74
Synthetic yarn	75–100[c]	15	100	---	51
Cotton fabrics	42.5–45[c]	100	100	---	41
Gunny bags	25[c]	91	99	---	68
Cement	70	87	100	1	27
Plate glass	40[c]	45	100	---	30
Electric bulbs	45	73	82	---	23

[c]Indicates controlled import.

Source: Economic Commission for Asia and the Far East, *Economic Survey of Asia and the Far East: 1963* (New York: United Nations, 1964), p. 41.

15. See Table 8.

"In China (Taiwan) the industrial units which rely heavily on imported raw materials for manufacturing finished goods, such as textiles, paper, iron and steel, and rubber products, have decided to export a stipulated percentage of their production. Failure to reach an export target exposes the industry to the payment of a fine or to closing down the proportion of a certain portion of its production capacity."[16]

Even so, however, as far as the trend is concerned, the fact that the proportion of finished consumption goods in total imports is declining, and the fact that there has been a remarkable increase in the proportion of exports occupied by manufactured goods (Table 9) are indications that, with some exceptions, industrialization as a whole is pressing steadily forward, centered on the import substitute industries.

In this way not only has there been an increase in the domestic consumption of agricultural products, including raw

Table 9: Composition of Exports and Imports

Period	Export				Import		
	Agricultural Products (%)	Processed Agricultural Products (%)	Industrial Products (%)	Others (%)	Capital Goods (%)	Agricultural & Industrial Raw Materials (%)	Consumption Goods (%)
1952	26.9	68.3	3.6	1.2	13.1	74.2	12.7
1953	13.1	79.6	6.4	0.9	17.3	68.6	14.1
1954	14.8	77.3	6.8	1.1	19.3	69.1	11.6
1955	29.7	62.6	6.1	1.6	18.6	71.2	10.2
1956	15.0	71.7	11.9	1.4	24.1	68.0	7.9
1957	16.6	74.7	7.2	1.5	26.4	65.8	7.8
1958	23.8	63.1	11.3	1.8	25.9	62.9	11.2
1959	24.0	53.6	20.9	1.5	31.1	61.2	7.7
1960	11.7	55.9	30.4	2.0	27.5	63.0	9.5
1961	15.3	42.7	39.7	2.3	28.4	59.7	11.9
1962	13.8	36.0	47.2	3.0	25.7	64.6	9.7
1963	14.3	43.1	39.5	3.1	24.6	67.0	8.4
1964	15.9	40.5	39.9	3.7	25.0	64.5	10.5
1965	25.2	29.5	41.3	4.0	29.5	62.7	7.8

Source: *Taiwan Statistical Data Book*, 1966, pp. 123 and 126.

---

16. *Economic Survey of Asia and the Far East: 1963, op. cit.,* p. 70.

materials, and in the processing of agricultural products, but there has also been a marked increase in the degree of dependence on imported agricultural products, chiefly in the form of increased imports of raw cotton and wheat. Indices for the production of food-stuffs and agricultural products in the period 1961-62 taking 1953-54 as the base, were 136 and 136 respectively, while import quantity indices for these goods were 140 and 153 respectively, higher figures in both cases. On the other hand, during the same period the index of domestic production in manufacturing industry stood at 231, while that of imported quantities of manufactured goods stood at 209, a lower rate of increase than that of production.

d) Fourth, progress in agriculture took place as a premise for the advance of the industrialization which I have described above. Land reform in particular contributed to this progress. I have already stated that the rate of growth in agricultural production was less than that of industry, but no development of industry can take place without progress in agriculture. This is because, in general, it is advantageous for the development of a country's industry if the domestic demand for industrial products has reached a certain scale. It is principally agriculture which forms this domestic demand. In the case of Taiwan, land reform was carried out in three stages, 1) the reduction of rents under the 37.5 per cent Farm Rent Limitation measure of 1948, which decreed that no more than 37.5 per cent of the principal product of the main crops could be taken as rent from land cultivated in tenancy; 2) the sale of public land to the peasants which began in 1951. This public land was confiscated agricultural land which had belonged to the Japanese government, Japanese commercial interests, or individual Japanese subjects before the war; and 3) the sale to the peasants of land owned by landlords, which began in 1953 under the Land-to-the-Tiller Program. Under this landlords' holdings in excess of three hectares were bought up by the government and sold to tenant cultivators.

This farm land policy was one of the traditional policies of the central government which moved to Taiwan from mainland China. These policies were implemented one after the other under the urgent necessity of taking steps deemed conducive to social stability. As much as possible of the great increase in population at the time was being absorbed by the agricultural sector.

As a result of this, there was a sharp decrease in the area of agricultural land cultivated in tenancy—from 38.6 per cent before the implementation of the land reform to 15.2 per cent after the implementation of the land reform.[17] As I have already stated, the number of peasant households increased to almost double the prewar figure. This caused a severe decline in the figures for area of cultivated land per household, but on the other hand, the yields of all crops were raised by intensive cultivation, the use of more labor and fertilizers, etc., and an increase in the varieties of crops raised. The ECAFE annual report speaks of this matter in the following terms:

"From 1948 to 1961 agricultural yield per unit land area increased by 4 per cent per annum, with two, three, four, or even five crops a year on the same plot of land. At present, gross agricultural output per hectare is the third highest in the world. Many new agricultural products which had never been produced on the island were introduced. From 1953-54 to 1961-62, agricultural output increased by 4.5 per cent per annum. This is faster than in any other ECAFE country including Japan. Such a rate of growth was made possible by the reform of 1953 which, by redistributing land to tillers, gave them incentives to improve productivity."[18]

Government research and the propagation of its results among the peasants of course contributed to this increase in agricultural production, and accompanied the development of the related fertilizer and insecticide industries.

However, more general in its effect was the provision of the pre-conditions for the development of domestic industry, particularly the production of consumer goods, by the increase in incomes in the agricultural sector which resulted from this expansion of agricultural production. Over the period 1952–

---

17. Hui-sun Tang, *Land Reform in Free China*, 1954, p. 138.
18. *Economic Survey of Asia and the Far East: 1963*, op. cit., p. 24.

61, the agricultural population remained at about 60 per cent of total employed population while agricultural incomes accounted for about 33 per cent of net national product, but one may suppose that the purchasing power of the agricultural population provided the major part of the market for the domestic consumer goods industries. At the end of the World War II the demand for textiles, together with that for food, was strong, as is shown by the Taipei wholesale price index for 1949, based on 1937 prices. The figure for textiles is much higher than that for food, and the textile industry was established as a domestic industry catering to a large and strong domestic demand in all areas of the nation. Since that time Taiwan's industries have been gradually diversified to include durable consumer goods such as electric fans, bicycles, etc., and intermediate goods, such as chemical products and building materials. In the background of these developments one must suspect the existence of a corresponding enlargement of the domestic market for the products of these industries. One may suppose that in regard to this enlargement of the domestic market the development of agricultural production was at least a powerful support.

Conclusion

I may summarize the foregoing by saying that economic growth in Taiwan is proceeding more or less steadily, centered on an industrialization that is supported by all kinds of economic aid. Let us review this process of growth.

a) First, the basic conditions which made possible the high rate of economic growth were an energetic people and investment in the human factor constituted thereby, the existence of fairly ample investments in social overhead capital, etc., so that the favorable external economies were already prepared before the economic construction plans were put into effect. This attribute was a valuable asset for Taiwan's economic development, nor was it one which could easily be acquired by other countries in a short space of time.

In the case of Taiwan one may even have grounds for thinking that the sudden rise in the population has had a positive significance, rather than the reverse, in that it has provided the large number of industries newly introduced into Taiwan with a rich source of young and adaptable labor. Although there is no statistical evidence, one may suppose that these many newly introduced industries have been able to achieve comparatively smooth growth because of this supply of young labor from the increase in the population. The transfer of labour from older industries to new industries is not necessarily an easy matter, nor is such labor necessarily efficient when transferred. New industries require not only an additional amount of labor but also new kinds of ability that can be found only in the lower age groups.

b) Second, I must mention the economic aid from the United States and the implementation of a thorough-going planned economy in a certain sense. The aid from the United States did not merely produce a corresponding furtherance of capital formation in terms of scale. It also made possible selective and thoroughly planned investment in important industries. The aid from the United States was actually granted on the understanding that it would be invested in specific projects which were considered likely to contribute to economic development. Again, economic planning was carried out in a thorough-going manner in all fields—in investment allocation, in price control, and in exchange and foreign trade control—and this was made possible by the fact that Taiwan is a small island country in which administrative control can be easily effected. As a result of this, the discrepancies between investment plans and performance have been of a degree of smallness seldom found in other countries. At least as far as the implementation of investment plans is concerned, these have been carried out successfully.

c) Third, the selection of industries and the selection of priorities with respect to these investments were comparatively rational. In general, countries which are small from the point of view of population and of per capita incomes are incapable of developing successfully those industries which require mass production and in which the industry or the unit of production cannot be sub-divided. Again, industries which from the first are designed only for export production are not successful. In this sense, Taiwan first took steps to restore and expand the existing basic industries—the energy and fertilizer industries, etc.—and by so doing provided for the development of agricultural production.

Further, as this expanded the domestic market, steps were taken to foster and develop new industries as import substitute industries catering to the increasing demand for certain commodities. Consequently, in the case of Taiwan it was impossible to choose industries requiring the investment of vast sums, such as large-scale steel production or ship-building. Thus, the industries actually chosen have been those in which the scale of production was relatively small and which entailed few difficulties in matters of technology as well as in other respects, such as the chemical industry in all its forms and the production of light machinery, electrical appliances, etc., dependent on imported intermediate goods. In these industries it was comparatively easy to find the small number of skilled workers required. In regard to the chemical industry the ECAFE annual report evaluates its positive role as follows. "In China (Taiwan) in the late 1950's a beginning was made in chemical industries. . . and these have once been considered a possible cluster for starting a new wave of development. In these industries, value added is large in relation to the cost of material, and they should be suitable for countries lacking adequate natural resources. Key factors required are techniques and initial capital, including foreign exchange."[19] I have already noted that steps are being taken to bring about a positive introduction of foreign capital.

---

19. *Economic Survey of Asia and the Far East: 1963, op. cit.,* p. 25.

d) However, in the fourth place there are the problems of the future. Since the domestic market is small, industries established with a view to substituting for imports are at once faced by the necessity of exporting, and at the present moment a certain section of industry is engaged in the export trade. There are two problems in this matter. The first is that of equality, and the other that of costs. Even if there are some problems regarding these two points, industries carried on under the protection of import restrictions and tariffs are capable of substituting exports for imports to some extent, but they must face stern competition if they go on to enter the export market.

On this point there is a stern view which holds that, leaving aside agricultural products based on Taiwan's natural resources,[20] it is doubtful whether Taiwan's industries will be of sufficient stature to stand up to foreign competition. It certainly seems that those of Taiwan's industries which require a high degree of skill and large-scale production are to be put to a stern test in international competition in the future, in regard to both quality and costs.

In regard to the lowering of costs, Taiwan's industries are at present much characterized by isolation and dispersal, and lack of mutual connection among them is considered an obstacle to this, and in this sense it is necessary, beyond the rationalization of individual enterprises and industries, to make further improvements in the external economies throughout the whole of industry. In the short term it would not be impossible to discover markets for "cheap and nasty" commodities of low quality and price among the other developing countries, but in the long term improvement of quality and lowering of costs are unavoidable. In this sense the economy of Taiwan, which has undergone a rapid industrialization centered on the import substitute industries, may be said to have come to a turning-point.

---

20. For example, pineapple, etc., and such chemical products industries as the cement, the fertilizer and seasonings industries, whose products are determined in the natural course of events by their technical processes of production in respect to their quality and rating.

Finally, I have to note that, even after 1965 when aid from the United States was terminated, Taiwan is experiencing a comparatively high economic growth rate. (Table 3.) This might be considered to show that Taiwan has already established her relatively stable ground as an industrializing country, although one cannot deny the profitable circumstances such as the expanded export market caused by the war in Vietnam.

4.

Key Factors in the Development of Thailand

Katsumi Mitani

The Author

KATSUMI MITANI writes about the economy of Thailand from the vantage point of extensive first-hand experience. As an economist with the Japanese Ministry of Finance, Mr. Mitani was transferred in 1959 to the Japan External Trade Organization and spent five years in Bangkok studying the Thai economy. He returned to the Ministry of Finance in 1962 and then joined the Japan Economic Research Institute in 1964 as Manager of the Research Division. In 1967–68, Mr. Mitani was a Visiting Scholar at Resources for the Future, Inc., in Washington, D.C., exploring the feasibility of employing nuclear power in developing countries. Mr. Mitani is a graduate of Kansai University, and the author of *International Balance of Payments and the Growth of Japan* and *The History of Japanese Emigrants to the United States in the Meiji Era.*

Mr. Mitani drafted his paper on the economy of Thailand as a member of a task force set up by Keizai Doyukai, CED's counterpart organization in Japan. The Chairman of the Task Force on Thailand's Economy was Tatsuzo Mizukami, President, Mitsui & Co., and the members of the group besides Mr. Mitani were: Ryokichi Hirono, Assistant Professor, Seikei University; Kohei Hotta, Deputy Representative for the Philippines, Bank of Tokyo; Hidematsu Kashima, Sub-Manager, Planning Department, Mitsui & Co.; Kiyoshi Kitamura, Planning Department, Mitsui & Co.; Mitsuaki Noguchi, Deputy Manager, Foreign Department, Mitsui Bank; Takeharu Sasamoto, Chief, Research Division, Institute of Asian Economic Affairs; Shuhei Togashi, Assistant Manager, Foreign Department, Mitsui Bank; Saburo Ueki, Assistant to the Chief, Economic Research Division, Bank of Japan.

Contents

Introduction — 163

Conditions Making for Economic Stability — 165
    Sound Monetary and Fiscal Policy — 168
    Export Expansion — 173
    Foreign Aid and Investment — 175
    Prospects for Economic Development — 180

Adaptation of Education to Development Needs — 182
    Development of Modern Education in Thailand — 183
    Impact on Consumption Patterns — 186
    The Educational Policy of the Thai Government — 193
        Primary Education — 195
        Secondary Education — 195
        Teacher Training — 195
        Higher Education — 196

The Role of the Thai-Chinese — 197

Foreign Private Investment and Economic Development — 201
    State Enterprises and Industrial Development of Thailand — 201
    Industrial Development Under the Sarit and Kittikachorn Governments — 202
    Foreign Capital and Industrial Development of Thailand — 205

Tables

1:	Gross National Product of Thailand, 1951–63	166
2:	Gold and Foreign Exchange Reserves	167
3:	Ratio of Gold and Foreign Exchange Reserves to Notes in Circulation and Imports	168
4:	Government Revenue and Expenditure, 1942–66	169
5:	Total Money Supply	171
6:	Ratio of Total Cash to Deposits in Commercial Banks, 1946–66	172
7:	Principal Exports	174
8:	Total Value of Trade	176
9:	Imports by Commodity Groups	177
10:	Balance of Payments, 1963–65	178
11:	Literacy Rate by Age Group	185
12:	Average Monthly Family Expenditures, 1962	190
13:	Family Ownership of Selected Durable Goods, 1962	191
14:	Sectoral Allocations of Development Expenditures Under the First and Second Development Plans	196
15:	Growth in Output of Chief Manufactured Goods, 1956–66	205
16:	Japanese Share of Thailand's Total Trade	208
17:	Share of Thailand's Total Exports of Primary Products Going to Japan, 1957–65	209
Appendix Table:	Number of Firms Opening or Adding New Facilities and Their Estimated Capital Expenditures	212

Introduction

Thanks to its traditionally sound monetary and fiscal policy, Thailand has been able, during the postwar years, to maintain a rapid economic growth without inflation. The exchange rate of the Thai currency (the baht) has been consistently firm.

Several Southeast Asian countries have been unable to achieve even a start on economic development because of political instability and unrest arising from the movement of these countries from colonial status to independence after World War II. Thailand was never colonized by a European power, and, though several revolutions have taken place, the changes in government have not caused social unrest or economic confusion. Since October 1958, when the late Field Marshal Sarit succeeded in a coup d'etat, the military has been in power. The constitution and national elections have been suspended, martial law has been in force, and the revolutionary government has maintained a stern anti-communist policy both internally and externally. Thailand's economy has shown remarkable progress during this period. This has helped to strengthen the confidence of the Thai people in their government, which in turn has contributed to a further stabilization of the military regime.

Although a number of restrictions have been placed on the political activity among the people of Thailand, their economic activity in general has been left extremely free of government control, aside from such measures as the ban on imports from Communist China. Various developing countries of Southeast Asia have attempted since World War II to set up comprehensive economic plans and regulate the allocation of development funds. Thailand did not embark on economic development until 1961, and in doing so, put the main emphasis on the development of agriculture and social overhead capital; the private initiative of both Thai and foreign enterprises has been relied on for the industrial development of the country. Thailand in recent years has put particular emphasis on encouraging foreign capital to come in through the granting of many privileges for industrial promotion.

The illiteracy rate in Thailand has been greatly reduced by many years of government effort to develop education. Such educational development has been instrumental also in promoting a desire for modern living among the Thai people. The development of vocational and technical education, though still inadequate in extent and quality, has made it possible for Thailand to supply technical and managerial manpower required in modern industry.

Over the past hundred years, the descendants of the Chinese who migrated to Thailand have been assimilated into Thai society. After the Communist came to power in China, the Thai Chinese stopped remitting their money home and began investing it in Thai industry. As a result, the Chinese population in Thailand now are active not only in their traditional commercial sector but also in the modern industrial sector of the country.

Thailand had long been behind in the highway construction and other social overhead investments, but since the war these facilities have been rapidly developed, principally through foreign aid and cooperation. This development of the infrastructure, along with the government's effort to promote industry, has improved the investment climate in Thailand and made the country more attractive to Chinese, Japanese, and other foreign private capital. Since 1960 there has been a rapid inflow of foreign private capital accompanied by modern technology.

Despite these favorable developments in Thailand since the war, several important problems also have emerged that require for their solution more intensive efforts on the part of the people and of the government of Thailand, as well as more international assistance and cooperation. Three major problem areas can be identified:

The country's export potential has been reduced by a slow increase in the population. Meanwhile, export prices of natural rubber have been rather unstable. These trends have created some uneasiness about future export earnings and consequently about the prospects for Thailand's international balance of payments.

While the loosening up of hoarded currency has thus far enabled Thailand to sustain rapid economic progress, continual growth will require a more flexible fiscal and monetary policy, together with the development of a better financial system.

The industrialization of Thailand in recent years has been phenomenal in terms both of expansion and diversification. However, Thailand must now gradually strengthen its protected import-substitution industries so that they can become competitive on the international market. Many problems will lie ahead, and the solution to these problems will obviously call for a great deal of effort on the part of everyone concerned, with the help of assistance and cooperation from abroad.

Conditions Making for Economic Stability

Due to their increasing expenditures for economic development, developing countries typically experience inflationary price increases and a continued deficit in their international balance of payments. In this respect, Thailand has been a rather conspicuous exception. Since World War II, the country has managed to achieve a relatively fast economic growth of over 7 per cent per annum on the average, at the same time maintaining a general price stability and a favorable

Table 1: Gross National Product of Thailand, 1951-63

Year	GNP (millions of baht)	GNP (millions of U.S. dollars)	Population (millions)	Per Capita GNP (baht)	Per Capita GNP (U.S. dollars)	Annual Rate of Increase GNP %	Annual Rate of Increase Population %	Annual Rate of Increase Per Capita GNP %	GNP at 1956 Constant Prices (millions of baht)	Annual Rate of Increase %
1951	28,219.8	1,343.8	20.3	1,390	66.2	—	—	—	31,214.5	—
1952	29,548.5	1,407.1	20.9	1,414	67.3	4.7	3.0	1.7	32,853.1	5.2
1953	32,164.5	1,531.6	21.5	1,496	71.2	8.9	2.9	5.8	35,484.4	8.0
1954	31,997.3	1,523.7	22.1	1,448	69.0	-0.5	2.8	-3.2	35,396.7	-0.2
1955	39,334.0	1,881.1	22.8	1,725	82.5	22.9	3.2	19.1	40,123.8	13.4
1956	40,928.9	1,981.1	23.5	1,742	84.3	4.1	3.1	1.0	40,928.9	2.0
1957	41,835.7	2,001.7	24.2	1,729	82.7	2.2	3.0	-0.7	41,290.8	0.9
1958	43,432.0	2,058.3	24.9	1,744	82.7	3.8	2.9	0.9	42,607.4	3.2
1959	48,338.1	2,281.1	25.6	1,888	89.1	11.3	2.8	8.2	47,282.6	10.9
1960	55,090.5	2,605.9	26.4	2,087	98.7	13.9	3.1	10.5	53,642.4	13.4
1961	58,087.2	2,767.3	27.2	2,136	101.7	5.4	3.0	2.3	55,553.0	3.6
1962	63,030.2	3,024.4	28.0	2,251	108.0	8.5	2.9	5.4	58,166.6	4.7
1963	67,609.9	3,244.2	28.8	2,348	112.6	7.3	2.9	4.3	64,167.0	10.3
(Average)						7.71	2.97	4.6		6.28

Notes: (1) Both the GNP and the per capita GNP figures are shown in current prices.
(2) Dollar equivalents of the GNP and the per capita GNP figures are computed. The exchange rate used for the period 1951-54 is 21 baht for one United States dollar; for the period after 1954 the going rates were used.

Sources: *Statistical Yearbook,* 1963, pp. 362 and 363; Bank of Thailand, *Monthly Report* (November 1965), pp. 70 and 72.

balance of payments. From 1951 to 1963, total gross national product (GNP) increased at the rate of 7.7 per cent per annum, and increase in per capita GNP averaged 4.6 per cent annually after allowing for the population increase of slightly less than 3 per cent a year over the same period. In constant prices, total GNP during those years showed an increase of approximately 6.3 per cent per annum. (See Table 1.)

The gold and foreign exchange reserves of Thailand rose from $296.9 million at the end of 1955 to $825.8 million at the end of 1966 (See Table 2). This was reflected in the improvement

Table 2: Gold and Foreign Exchange Reserves
(thousands of U. S. dollars)

Year	Gold	Foreign Exchange	Total	Exchange Rates (baht per U. S. dollar)	Total (millions of baht)
1955	112,458	184,486	296,944	21.40	6,355
1956	112,458	198,840	311,298	20.66	6,431
1957	112,457	206,544	319,001	20.90	6,667
1958	112,457	187,299	299,756	21.10	6,325
1959	104,332	193,561	297,893	21.19	6,312
1960	104,332	238,446	342,778	21.14	7,246
1961	104,203	317,109	421,312	20.99	8,843
1962	104,203	379,410	483,613	20.84	10,078
1963	104,203	425,020	529,223	20.84	11,029
1964	104,203	494,104	598,307	20.84	12,468
1965	96,453	576,099	672,552	20.83	14,009
1966	91,703	734,140	825,843	20.75	17,136

Source: Bank of Thailand, *Monthly Report* (March 1967), p. 12.

in the exchange rate of the baht from 21.40 baht to the United States dollar in 1955 to 20.75 baht in 1966, as of the year-end in each case. The foreign exchange reserves of Thailand at the end of 1966 (17.1 billion baht), were greater than the total amount of bank notes in circulation (11.0 million baht) at that time, and these reserves were more than sufficient to cover Thai imports over a period of 10 months at the current rate. (See Table 3).

Such an extremely healthy state in the international balance of payments is rarely found among the developing countries in the world.

168 KEY FACTORS IN THE DEVELOPMENT OF THAILAND

Table 3: Ratio of Gold and Foreign Exchange Reserves to Notes in Circulation and Imports
(millions of baht)

Year	Gold & Foreign Exchange Reserves (1)	Notes in Circulation (2)	Imports Total	Imports Monthly Average (3)	(1) ÷ (2)	(1) ÷ (3)
1955	6,355	5,543	7,503	625	1.15	10.17
1956	6,431	5,802	7,655	638	1.11	10.08
1957	6,667	5,993	8,537	711	1.11	9.38
1958	6,325	5,864	8,237	686	1.08	9.22
1959	6,312	6,249	8,988	749	1.10	8.43
1960	7,246	6,661	9,622	802	1.09	9.03
1961	8,843	7,268	10,287	857	1.22	10.32
1962	10,078	7,414	11,504	959	1.36	10.51
1963	11,029	7,741	12,803	1,066	1.42	10.35
1964	12,468	8,474	14,253	1,188	1.47	10.49
1965	14,009	9,379	16,185	1,348	1.49	10.39
1966	17,136	11,055	—	—	1.55	—

Source: Bank of Thailand, *Monthly Report* (March 1967), p. 5, 12, and 27.

Sound Monetary and Fiscal Policy

The stability of the Thai economy can be attributed in large measure to the sound monetary and fiscal policy carried out by the monetary authorities and the government of Thailand.

Between 1942 and 1957 the government enjoyed a surplus for the most part. Since 1958, when the late Field Marshal Sarit succeeded in a coup d'etat, there has been a deficit annually. (See Table 4.)

The rapid increase in capital expenditure by the Revolutionary Government has resulted in an unbalanced annual budget. However, the expansionary budget expenditures have contributed on the one hand to providing an infrastructure for the country and promoting economic growth, while strict monetary measures have been maintained on the other hand. If the deficit can be limited to an amount which would have a "moderate" inflationary effect upon the economy, the fiscal policy will continue to be still sound in the case of a developing country like Thailand.

Table 4: Government Revenue and Expenditure, 1942–66

Fiscal Year	Revenue Baht (thousands)	Revenue Rate of Increase (per cent)	Expenditure Baht (thousands)	Expenditure Rate of Increase (per cent)	Balance (baht thousands) Surplus	Balance (baht thousands) Deficit
1942	133,176	–	146,051	–	–	12,874
1943	211,584	58.9%	146,179	0.1%	65,405	–
1944	288,905	36.5	254,671	74.2	34,235	–
1945	315,610	9.2	264,187	3.7	51,423	–
1946	626,294	98.4	475,642	80.0	150,652	–
1947	996,063	59.1	539,729	13.5	456,334	–
1948	1,691,640	69.8	1,582,764	193.3	108,876	–
1949	1,929,741	14.1	1,695,753	7.1	233,989	–
1950	2,136,099	10.7	2,078,709	22.6	57,390	–
1951	2,531,156	18.5	2,445,692	17.7	85,464	–
1952	3,347,403	32.2	3,371,806	37.9	–	24,403
1953	3,942,033	17.8	3,850,162	14.2	91,871	–
1954	4,239,938	7.6	4,251,694	10.4	–	11,756
1955	4,185,444	1.3	3,999,111	5.9	186,333	–
1956	5,080,760	21.4	4,549,341	13.8	531,420	–
1957	5,198,516	2.3	4,948,539	8.8	249,977	–
1958	5,616,049	8.0	6,019,280	21.6	–	403,231
1959	6,055,195	7.8	7,077,465	17.6	–	1,022,270
1960	6,786,421	12.1	7,586,563	7.2	–	800,142
1961	5,689,946	16.2	6,314,653	16.8	–	624,708
1962	7,986,223	40.4	8,641,790	36.9	–	655,567
1963	8,633,136	8.1	9,624,681	11.4	–	991,546
1964	9,655,522	11.9	10,949,636	13.8	–	1,294,115
1965	11,066,000	12.7	12,525,000	14.4	–	1,459,000
1966	12,525,000	13.2	14,523,000	15.9	–	1,998,000

Notes: Up to 1961, the fiscal year coincided with the calendar year. Thereafter, it was changed to October 1 of one year to September 30 of the following year. The fiscal year 1961, therefore, covers only a nine-month period beginning on January 1, 1961 and ending on September 30, 1961.

Sources: *Statistical Yearbook, 1965*, p. 389; Bank of Thailand, *Annual Economic Report*, 1966, pp. 29-32.

A conservative monetary policy has indeed been maintained. Any increase in the issuance of Central Bank notes has been limited by and large to an increase in the foreign exchange resources available to the government. As a result, between 1954 and 1963, Central Bank notes increased from 4,548.3 million baht to 6,703.5 million baht in circulation. (See Table 5.) Against this 47.4 per cent increase, the GNP rose 111.3 per cent over the same period.

To supplement this low rate of increase in currency, which was even less than a half the rate of expansion in the national output, there had been a huge increase in demand deposits held by the public. Total demand deposits between 1954 and 1963 increased from 1,888.3 million to 5,177.5 million baht, a rise of 174.2 per cent. Thus, the ratio of cash to demand deposits changed from 2.4 in 1954 to 1.3 in 1963. The total money supply (i.e., the total volume of currency and demand deposits held by the public) therefore expanded by 84.6 per cent, approaching the rate of increase in GNP during the same period. However, it is to be noted that the money market of Bangkok, the capital and the financial center of Thailand, has long been maintained in a tight condition. Thus, on the one hand Thailand has been able to maintain since the war a continuous economic stability, while on the other hand the phenomenal increase in the total volume of demand deposits has helped make possible a remarkable economic expansion.

In prewar Thailand there were only three Thai banks and six foreign-owned banks. The latter were responsible in the main for international transactions, while the former were for domestic financing. Much of the domestic financial transactions were carried out by such overseas Chinese financing agencies as Yin-Shing-Shu, which handled foreign remittances, and by such personal finance associations as Hsing-pang, which operated pawn shops, and Chin-Hang, which was in the jewelry business. The masses of the Thai people had little faith in these banking institutions, and virtually no incentive to save.

It was only after the war that banking institutions began to develop in Thailand. The enactment of the Commercial Banking Act of 1945 brought about a very rapid growth of commercial

Table 5: Total Money Supply

(millions of baht)

Year	GNP (1) GNP	GNP (1) Rate of Increase (per cent)	Currency (2) Held by Public	Currency (2) Rate of Increase (per cent)	Demand Deposits (3) Held by Public	Demand Deposits (3) Rate of Increase (per cent)	Money Supply (2) + (3) Total	Money Supply (2) + (3) Rate of Increase (per cent)
1954	31,997.3	0.5%	4,548.3	—	1,888.3	—	6,436.6	—
1955	39,334.0	22.9	5,178.7	13.9%	2,048.3	8.5%	7,227.0	12.3%
1956	40,928.9	4.1	5,424.1	4.7	2,304.3	12.5	7,728.4	6.9
1957	41,835.7	2.2	5,573.0	2.7	2,623.6	13.9	8,196.6	6.1
1958	43,432.0	3.8	5,504.0	1.2	2,947.9	12.4	8,451.9	3.1
1959	48,338.1	11.3	5,784.6	5.1	3,291.5	11.7	9,076.1	7.4
1960	55,090.5	13.9	6,048.9	4.6	4,039.5	22.7	10,088.4	11.2
1961	58,087.2	5.4	6,511.7	7.7	4,563.7	13.0	11,075.4	9.8
1962	63,030.2	8.5	6,573.4	0.9	4,519.9	1.0	11,093.3	0.2
1963	67,609.9	7.3	6,703.5	2.0	5,177.5	14.5	11,881.0	7.1
Increase from 1954–1963		111.3%		47.4%		174.2%		84.6%

Source: Bank of Thailand, *Monthly Report* (November 1965).

banks, from 32 offices in 1954 to 512 in November 1966. There was also a gradual development of government-owned savings banks and institutions. People's increasing faith in banks resulted in the rapid expansion of bank deposits. With the extension of the monetized economy, the enlargement of commodity markets, and the further development of the banking institutions, the hoarded currency has been gradually absorbed by these banking institutions and circulated throughout the national economy.

The main function of the commercial bank, the creation of credit, also has become increasingly important in Thailand. This is evidenced by the fact that the amount of cash on hand plus the balances carried by commercial banks with the Bank of Thailand has declined as a ratio of time and demand deposits from a high of 58.7 per cent in 1946 to a low of 8.1 per cent in 1966. (See Table 6). This again demonstrates that pro-

Table 6: Ratio of Total Cash to Deposits in Commercial Banks, 1946–66 (in December of each year)

Year	Ratio (per cent)	Year	Ratio (per cent)
1946	58.74%	1956	19.67%
1947	40.11	1957	19.17
1948	44.25	1958	15.24
1949	39.31	1959	16.36
1950	38.99	1960	14.68
1951	36.13	1961	15.16
1952	30.97	1962	13.73
1953	29.41	1963	13.46
1954	25.74	1964	10.98
1955	20.06	1965	9.20
		1966	8.09

Notes: Total cash means cash on hand and balances with the Bank of Thailand. Deposits include both demand and time deposits.
Sources: Bank of Thailand, *Monthly Report* (March 1967), pp. 8 and 9.

vision of the modern banking facilities has been responsible in a major way for the remarkable economic growth of Thailand during the postwar years.

Export Expansion

In contrast to those countries in Southeast Asia that require a sizable sum of foreign exchange every year to import foodstuff, Thailand exports a large volume of rice and earns a considerable amount of foreign currency every year. During the early postwar years there was an acute food shortage in many areas around the world, but later the shortage began to slacken and a downward trend set in for food prices. Throughout the entire postwar period, however, the price of rice has stayed at a relatively high level in international transactions, and this has contributed in turn to a high level of export earnings for Thailand.

Thailand's production of rice has also been relatively steady during the postwar period. Thailand's geographic situation, particularly its long stretch from north to south, reduces the possibility that there could be poor crop conditions on a nationwide scale. True, the country did suffer from a bad crop in 1958, but Thailand was not hit as hard as some other countries of Southeast Asia, which had to import a huge quantity of foodstuffs. The consequence for Thailand was merely a reduction in the amount or rice exported abroad that year. Nevertheless, from a long-range point of view, the fact that rice cultivation has begun to be extended into northeastern provinces of Thailand, where land is relatively ill-suited to such cultivation, seems to indicate that rice production will have approached a plateau in the near future.

Thailand's rapid export expansion since the war has been due both to rising world demand for its traditional items of export as well as to the country's development of new export products. The total value of exports of the four principal products that traditionally comprised the bulk of Thailand's export trade—rice, rubber, tin and teak—more than doubled between 1951 and 1965. (See Table 7.) However, whereas these items accounted for more than 80 per cent of Thailand's total exports in the early 1950's, by 1965 they accounted for only a little more than half the total exports. Beginning in the mid-1950's, there was a rapid development of several new export

174 KEY FACTORS IN THE DEVELOPMENT OF THAILAND

Table 7: Principal Exports

(millions of baht)

Year	Total Exports	Traditional Items of Export					Percentage of Total Exports	New Export Items				Percentage of Total Exports
		Rice	Rubber	Tin	Teak	Total		Maize	Tapioca Products	Jute and Kenaf	Total	
1951	4,413	1,824	1,469	187	158	3,638	82.4%	—	—	—	—	—
1952	4,619	2,629	1,009	224	97	3,959	85.7	—	—	—	—	—
1953	5,772	3,749	751	300	133	4,933	85.5	—	—	—	—	—
1954	6,177	3,087	1,109	374	211	4,781	77.4	—	—	—	—	—
1955	7,121	3,133	1,802	441	264	5,640	79.2	80	52[a]	11	143	2.0
1956	6,923	2,861	1,526	507	306	5,200	75.1	96	94[a]	19	209	3.0
1957	7,540	3,622	1,406	531	262	5,821	77.2	74	138	46	258	3.4
1958	6,447	2,968	1,326	255	239	4,788	74.3	183	192	69	444	6.9
1959	7,560	2,576	2,336	434	244	5,590	73.9	250	224	88	562	7.4
1960	8,614	2,570	2,579	537	356	6,042	70.1	551	287	230	1,068	12.4
1961	9,997	3,598	2,130	617	252	6,597	66.0	597	446	627	1,670	16.2
1962	9,529	3,240	2,111	685	170	6,206	65.1	502	423	579	1,504	15.6
1963	9,676	3,424	1,903	741	137	6,205	64.1	828	439	358	1,625	16.6
1964	12,339	4,389	2,060	962	179	7,590	61.5	1,346	653	495	2,494	20.2
1965	12,941	4,334	1,999	767	201	7,301	56.4	969	676	1,102	2,747	21.2

[a]Tapioca flour only.
Sources: Trade Statistics by Customs Office of Thailand; Bank of Thailand, *Monthly Reports* (March 1967), pp. 44 and 45.

items—maize, tapioca products, jute and kenaf—whose share of total exports rose from only 2 per cent in 1955 to 21.2 per cent in 1965. Jute and kenaf together now rank third in importance among Thai exports, after rice and rubber, while maize now ranks fourth. These have replaced tin in importance, while exports of tapioca products now exceed those of teak.

To sum up, while Thailand's export trade still depends heavily on a relatively few primary products, increased production of those items meeting changing demand overseas has helped Thailand to increase its export earnings in recent years and has thus contributed to the maintenance of its stable international balance of payment.

Foreign Aid and Investment

Thailand has experienced a continuous increase in imports during the postwar period because of the upgrading of mass-consumption patterns. On the one hand this has created a demand for consumer goods that are not produced locally and must be imported, and on the other hand it has stimulated the growth of domestic consumer-goods industries that must import capital equipment from abroad to increase production sufficiently to satisfy the increasing market. While the total volume of imports increased 2.5 times over a 12-year period, from 6,471 million baht in 1953 to 16,185 million baht in 1965, imports of machinery and equipment more than tripled during the same period, from 1,366 million baht to 4,924 million baht. (See Tables 8 and 9.)

As a consequence of this rapid import expansion, Thailand has been confronted with increasingly unfavorable trade balances since 1952. However, these deficits have been offset annually by foreign aid, and, particularly in recent years, by private foreign investments in addition to the foreign aid.

For example, in 1965 the annual deficit in the balance of trade amounted to 3,150 million baht, but in the same year Thailand received the foreign grants in the amount of 1,323.1 million baht and so-called "Special Yen" transfers (Japanese war reparations) equivalent to 58.2 million baht. (See Table 10.)

There has been an increase in total official transfer payments received by Thailand from 528.8 million baht in 1958 to 1,372.9 million baht in 1965, though the rise has not been steady from year to year. There has been also a notable increase since 1961 in the volume of foreign direct investment and long-term loans from private sources abroad. This is a reflection of the increased tempo of industrialization in Thailand.

Table 8: Total Value of Trade
(millions of baht)

Year	Exports	Imports	Balance
1953	5,693	6,471	−778
1954	6,105	7,021	−916
1955	7,009	7,502	−493
1956	6,716	7,655	−939
1957	7,540	8,537	−997
1958	6,447	8,237	−1,790
1959	7,560	8,988	−1,428
1960	8,614	9,622	−1,008
1961	9,997	10,287	−290
1962	9,529	11,504	−1,975
1963	9,676	12,803	−3,127
1964	12,339	14,253	−1,914
1965	12,941	16,185	−3,244
Percentage Increase 1953-65	127.3%	150.1%	

Sources: *Statistical Yearbook, 1963*; Bank of Thailand, *Monthly Report* (March 1967), pp. 27.

To illustrate, in 1965 Thailand received 590.8 million baht in the form of foreign direct investments and 516.6 million in the form of private loans from abroad. Combining these foreign investments and loans with the foreign grants and the "Special Yen" mentioned above yielded 2,488.7 million baht and nearly offset the trade deficit in 1965.

It has often been found that the foreign aid and loans received by some developing countries, regardless of the size of these funds, have contributed nothing to economic develop-

Table 9: Imports by Commodity Groups

(millions of baht)

Year	Total	Food	Minerals Fuels & Lubricants	Machinery	Raw Materials	Chemicals	Manufactured Goods	Others
1953	6,471	630	471	1,366	81	337	2,326	1,293
1954	7,021	639	567	1,388	83	526	2,582	1,234
1955	7,502	661	691	1,383	75	580	2,761	1,351
1956	7,655	111	775	1,522	79	654	2,977	1,037
1957	8,537	694	928	1,907	74	754	3,149	1,031
1958	8,237	781	901	1,861	72	757	2,964	901
1959	8,988	813	945	2,200	71	922	3,116	1,069
1960	9,622	784	1,025	2,390	143	974	3,289	1,118
1961	10,287	765	1,011	2,455	207	1,045	3,757	1,047
1962	11,504	755	1,224	3,156	205	1,190	3,872	1,102
1963	12,803	812	1,221	3,904	224	1,242	4,188	1,212
1964	14,253	876	1,458	4,520	282	1,486	4,343	1,288
1965	16,185	891	1,364	4,924	477	1,674	5,016	1,839
Percentage Increase 1953–65	150.1%	41.4%	189.6%	260.4%	488.8%	396.7%	115.6%	42.2%

Sources: *Statistical Yearbook, 1963*, p. 278; Bank of Thailand, *Monthly Report* (March 1967), p. 31.

Table 10:   Balance of Payments, 1963-65
(millions of baht)

Item	1963	1964	1965
A. Goods, Services and Private Transfer Payments			
Exports f.o.b.	9,577.7	12,165.0	12,663.5
Imports c.i.f.	−12,547.0	−14,022.2	−15,813.7
Trade balance	−2,969.3	−1,857.2	−3,150.2
Non-monetary gold	−147.7	−110.6	128.8
Freight and merchandise insurance	87.6	170.7	274.6
Other transportation	137.0	132.5	91.0
Travel	−148.6	−219.8	−149.8
Investment income	−40.4	−78.7	−11.1
Government n.i.e.	576.4	744.6	1,308.8
Other services	74.2	−16.7	−69.7
Private transfer payments	144.9	130.9	146.2
Total	−2,285.9	−1,104.3	−1,689.0
B. Official Transfer Payments			
Grants	944.8	601.3	1,323.1
Japanese war reparations	58.2	58.2	58.2
Rice donated to UNICEF and foreign countries	−2.6	−4.6	−2.4
Other	−7.1	−10.7	−6.0
Total	993.3	644.2	1,372.9
C. Capital Movements[a]			
Private			
Direct investment	354.0	374.2	590.8
Loans to gov't. enterprises:			
drawings	955.4	681.9	445.0
repayments	−249.5	−399.8	−426.4
Other private long-term	574.6	812.1	331.2
Other private short-term	−20.9	36.3	185.4
Central government			
Loans: drawings	52.5	328.1	331.7
repayments	−48.9	−57.4	−49.5
Long-term assets	−12.2	−18.1	−18.9
Other capital	40.0	−16.2	6.4
Total	1,645.0	1,650.2	1,395.7
D. Total (A through C)	352.4	1,197.3	1,079.6
E. Net Errors and Omissions	596.3	239.6	625.9
F. Monetary Movements	−948.7	−1,436.9	−1,705.5

[a]Other than monetary movements.
Source: Bank of Thailand, *Monthly Report* (March 1967), p. 51.

ment, and in some cases they even have proven detrimental. Economic development has not always been smooth in those "nonaligned" countries where the East and West seem to be competing in aid to curry favor. Moreover, in cases of massive military assistance, the social unrest that is created deters further economic development. These unfortunate consequences tend to ensue particularly when the foreign assistance corrupts politicians, bureaucrats, and military personnel in the receiving countries. There are also some developing countries that are being forced to float government bonds abroad to repay the principal and interest of the huge foreign loans obtained for their ambitious economic development plans. Thailand, however, differs in that foreign grants and loans have contributed greatly to the further development of the Thai economy. Their contribution has been outstanding, particularly in the construction of highways, harbor facilities, and dams, and in the development of power resources as well.[1]

The foregoing discussion of the effect of foreign aid on the economic development of developing countries seems to suggest that what is important is not the amount of foreign grants and loans available to developing countries but whether or not they possess the ability to make an effective use of those assistances from abroad. Too much foreign aid, if given to ill-equipped developing countries, would hamper a smooth development of

---

1. Great progress has been made in the development of electric power under the Six-Year Economic Development Plan beginning in 1961. Much of the expenditure for the power development in Thailand has come from abroad in the form of aid and loans. Of the total 2,341 million baht expended during 1961 to 1963 on the development of power, 1,515 million baht came from foreign loans, while foreign grants accounted for 169 million baht. A major portion of the foreign loans was allocated to the Yanhee project, the most ambitious power development ever undertaken in Thailand. Foreign loans and grants will also account for a large share of the total financing for the development of roads, transportation facilities, and communications. Of the total development expenditures of 32,657 million baht estimated for the 1961–66 period, 10,638 million baht came from foreign sources; the Second Five-Year Plan (1967–71) will require 14,435 million baht from foreign sources out of a totaled expenditures of 41,440 million baht. Thailand's highway system, while designed in large part for national defense, has contributed greatly to the economic development of adjacent areas.

their economies. Herein lies one major limitation of the foreign aid to developing countries.[2]

Prospects for Economic Development

Though there is no doubt up to now that the Thai economy has maintained stability, both domestically and externally, this does not preclude dangers that lie ahead.

First of all, there is an anxiety over the export potential of Thailand. Rice has been the foremost major item of Thai export during the prewar and postwar years. But the difficulty is that there has been a general decline in the rate of increase in rice production, compounded by a steady increase in population. These twin problems make it unlikely that Thailand will be able to maintain its current rate of rice export. At the same time there is also the likelihood that greater production and utilization of synthetic rubber throughout the world will push down the price of natural rubber. Since these two major commodities now constitute approximately a half of the total volume of Thai exports, it is possible that Thailand's export potential may be seriously impaired.

For this reason, Japan's cooperation and trade with Thailand has had a particular importance in that it has contributed in no small measure to the expansion and diversification of Thai exports.

The increase in Thailand's maize exports since 1958 is due principally to Japan's increased purchases. In spite of the fact that the United States has always been a supplier of cheap maize, Japan has helped Thailand increase its exports of maize

---

2. Thai economy has been affected by the war in Vietnam, especially in the last few years. The increased consumption by many Americans, both servicemen and civilians, together with the expenditure for the construction of military bases in Thailand, has given artificial stimulation to the economy through the absorption of both goods and services. In the northeastern area along the Laotian border the activities of the communist guerillas have been growing gradually; this has added to the economic fluctuations. If the escalation of the war in Vietnam should continue for a long period into the future, it could have an unfavorable influence upon the political and social stability of Thailand and could lead to an abnormal development of the economy.

through a partial guarantee of production. Japan also has provided assistance to Thailand on the improvement of drying facilities for maize to facilitate collection and storage of the product.

As a substitute for Pakistani jute, Japan has imported kenaf from Thailand, and thus helped to develop kenaf-producing areas in the remote northeast region of Thailand. Thailand's export of tapioca flour to Japan has also been on the increase. One Japanese firm manufacturing condiments has started production in Thailand, using as raw materials tapioca grown in the country. The tapioca-producing areas in the southeastern part of Thailand have been increasingly flourishing since around 1960.[3]

The importance of agriculture to the country's economy has been fully recognized by the government, which has given agriculture a prominent place in its two economic development plans. (The first plan was for the years 1961 to 1966, and the present plan runs from 1966 to 1971.) In order to promote the private initiative and development efforts for increased production, the government has been building the agricultural infrastructure, such as irrigation, power, and communications, and carrying out agricultural research and experimentation to improve crops and modernize farm techniques.

Aside from the need for further agricultural diversification, there is another problem facing Thailand that affects more broadly its over-all economic development. This concerns a reorientation of the monetary and fiscal policy traditionally maintained by Thailand. Up to now, as already noted, Thailand's economic growth has been facilitated by a growth in bank deposits. However, it seems unlikely that the ratio of cash to bank deposits can be compressed much more than the 8.09 per

---

3. It should also be noted that Japan has tried to develop imports from Thailand other than agricultural products. For instance, in seeking to increase its purchase of common salt from Thailand, Japan sent its technical personnel and helped to improve the quality of the Thai product. Thailand also has been able to mine its iron ore deposits with assistance of Japanese firms, and has already begun to earn some foreign exchanges by supplying the ore to Japanese iron and steel manufacturers.

cent ratio of 1966. Hence, it will be difficult for the commercial banks to increase greatly their lending capability. In this connection, it should be welcome that beginning in 1964 a somewhat more positive fiscal policy has been maintained by the Government of Thailand for its further economic development.

Development of a banking system outside commercial banking is yet to come in Thailand. The Bank of Thailand itself is limited in its functions, which have mainly involved currency issuance, foreign trade and exchange control, operation of the foreign-exchange stabilization account, and performance of the fiscal duties for the central government.

The bank has not come to perform the functions commonly carried on by central banks elsewhere, such as open-market operations and credit controls over city banks. The bank is also supposed to refinance export advances and rediscount drafts for advances on industrial raw materials, but not much has been done in this respect either. Thailand also lags in developing agricultural financing, long-term credit institutions, security markets, and other financial systems that promote the further development of an economy.

Adaptation of Education to Development Needs

In two respects, education plays a decisive role in furthering the economic development of a developing country.

First, education helps create a desire among the masses of people to change the existing social and cultural environments in which they live. It is only when a modern consumption pattern begins to prevail among the masses that a "traditional" society is formed and, to borrow W. W. Rostow's phrase, the "preconditions for a take-off" are developed. In Thailand, the majority of the people are farmers who have long maintained a tradition-bound, conservative way of life, with little contact with the outside world. Under such circumstances, extension of modern education has played a very important role in transforming this pattern of behavior among the Thai people.

Second, education plays a crucial role in the economic development of a country by supplying the necessary skilled manpower. Here the role of education is to train personnel of varied educational attainments and possessing different kinds of skill. The main drive for the economic development of a developing country is not the amount of development funds available to the country, but its ability to make an effective use of these funds. In other words, a developing country must have the capability to run the national economy, effectively administer public finance, and manage private business enterprise; together with the level of skill possessed by its workers, these are the key factors in economic development. Thailand has now grown to a stage where its further economic development requires countless scientific, engineering, and professional talents. To meet this manpower requirement, Thailand has to develop an appropriate manpower policy, and this obviously involves educational development.

Development of Modern Education in Thailand

Modern education in Thailand started during the reign of King Mongkut (1851-68), and these beginnings were advanced by his son King Chulalongkorn (1868-1910).[4] However, the national educational system of Thailand did not make rapid progress on account of financial difficulties and a shortage of

---

4. King Mongkut's name will be immediately recognized by all who are familiar with Margaret D. Landon's *Anna and the King of Siam.*
King Chulalongkorn founded a royal school in 1871 for the purpose of training princes and aristocrats to be modern bureaucrats. He also sent many princes abroad for study, and trained able government officials by establishing the King's Scholarship in 1897. In 1884 a plan was formulated to give educational opportunities to the general public. Three years later a bureau of education was founded in the government and promoted to a ministry in 1889.

teachers. As late as 1918–19, only 20 per cent of the male children of school age were enrolled.

The Primary Education Act was promulgated in 1921 and a four-year compulsory education was instituted for children between 7 and 14 years of age. The law first applied to about one-half of the 5,053 villages over the country, and its area of application was then gradually widened. In 1932 a constitutional revolution broke out, and the new revolutionary government, stressing public education under democracy, set up a nation-wide compulsory education system in 1935.[5]

As the proportion of children enrolled gradually rose, the literacy rate among the people of Thailand also increased.[6] There remained, however, a number of problems, such as shortages of teachers and educational facilities. The UNESCO Mission sent to Thailand in 1949 recommended that the length of the primary education in Thailand should be extended at the earliest possible time from four to eight years, including pre-school education, and that emphasis should be placed not only on the maintenance of the ability to read and write among the people but also on their acquisition of the minimum necessary qualification for a democratic nation.

Based on this recommendation, the government of the late Marshal Pibul drafted a new education plan in 1951, and attempts were made to improve vocational education, hitherto the weakest of all types of Thai education. Also, primary extension

---

5. In spite of a stipulation in the Primary Education Act that children start schooling at seven years of age, a majority of the children who entered the primary schools in 1935 had already reached nine to ten years of age. Thus, a change was initiated by the Ministry of Education to fix the age range of children in primary schools between eight and fifteen years of age, thus giving children ample time to complete primary education.
6. According to the 1947 census, 67 per cent of the children between 8 and 13 years of age were in the primary schools. However, every year there were a significant number of cases of student failure, retention, and repeating. The Ministry of Education reported in 1950 that only 26 per cent of those above 15 years of age had completed four years of compulsory education. Also, according to the 1937 census, the literacy rate among the male population over 10 years of age was reported to be 47 per cent, while 14.9 per cent was reported for the same age group of females. Ten years later, however, the census reported 67 per cent for the male and 40 per cent for the female population, showing a narrowing trend in the sex differential for the country.

Table 11: Literacy Rate by Age Group

Age Group	Number of People	Number Able to Read and Write	Literacy Rate Total	Men	Women
	(thousands)			(per cent)	
10-14	3,088	2,647	85.7	86.6	84.8
15-19	2,488	2,210	88.5	91.0	85.8
20-24	2,416	2,028	84.0	88.6	79.4
25-29	2,071	1,662	80.3	85.7	75.0
30-34	1,753	1,371	78.2	86.0	70.3
35-39	1,372	905	66.0	80.3	51.3
40-44	1,132	607	53.6	73.5	33.5
45-49	976	468	48.0	69.7	25.8
50-54	811	305	32.7	62.8	13.0
55-59	650	212	32.7	56.8	9.1
60-64	473	137	29.1	52.4	7.4
65 and over	734	175	23.9	46.1	6.2
Unknown	46	22	49.4	63.1	32.1
Total	18,026	12,756	70.8%	80.9%	61.0%

Source: Central Statistical Office (now National Statistical Office), National Economic Development Board, *Thailand Population Census 1960, Whole Kingdom,* p. 20.

schools were set up over the country as a preliminary step toward the extension of the primary education in the future.

The Thai government accepted assistance from the United States and other countries to promote the new education plan of 1951. United States assistance to education in Thailand began in 1951 as part of the Mutual Security Assistance Program, and has been continued under different names since then. Under the Thai-German Economic and Technical Cooperation Agreement, the Thai-German Vocational School was set up in 1956 to supply skilled and technical workers who would form part of "a healthy stock of middle classes" in Thailand. Japanese assistance was provided in 1960 to establish a telecommunications institute and train personnel in sophisticated communications technology. This was followed by another Japanese assistance program in 1964, establishing a training center in southern Thailand where Japanese experts are to teach highway engineering.

In addition to this aid from foreign countries for technical education in Thailand, various international organizations have also provided assistance. For example, the South East Asia Treaty Organization established the SEATO Graduate School of Engineering on the campus of Chulalongkorn University in Bangkok for the purpose of raising the level of technology in Southeast Asian countries. SEATO also has set up 17 technical schools all over the country; these are making a significant contribution in improving the level of technical knowledge and skills among the youth in Thailand. Furthermore, the number of Thai students studying abroad is not inconsiderable. It should be noted in passing that every year a number of Thai students, men and women, apply for the Japanese Government Scholarships to study in Japan. All these programs have helped raise the level of technical and general education in Thailand.

Impact on Consumption Patterns

During Thailand's long period of monarchial reign, the land and the people belonged to the king, while the aristocracy's function was to handle the national administration. The peasants were free men, who tilled as much of the king's land as they and their families could take care of. They gave the king part of their produce, and their labor was requisitioned by the aristocracy in the name of the king. There were also a large number of slaves in Thailand.

This social and economic structure underwent a radical change following the signing of the Bowring Treaty in 1855, granting full extraterritorial rights to Great Britain. But in their long history, the Thais never experienced the kind of feudal landownership pattern typical to Japan and the European countries, a fact that helps to explain some of the unique aspects of Thailand's later economic development.

As pointed out by Professor Tadeo Umesao of Kyoto University, the feudal system in Japan and Western Europe gave rise to the bourgeoisie, which in turn had a profound influence on the later development of capitalism. But in other parts of the world, the shift to capitalism was preceded not by the feudal system, but by autocratic monarchy or colonial rule. This prevented the growth of the bourgeoisie and the maturing of the capitalistic system, as in the case of Thailand.

In this connection, the remarks of Dr. James C. Ingram are particularly interesting:

"A conspicuous fact seen in Thailand since 1850 is that the Thais usually left the entrepreneur role in the hands of foreigners. They rarely engaged themselves not only in broker business but also in industrial management and all other activities requiring entrepreneurial initiative and imagination."

The rapid diffusion of modern education since World War II, however, has served to build up among the Thais a sound individualistic spirit necessary in a modern society. Thanks to the development of education, the Thai people have come to acquire the requisite qualities and attributes for managers running modern enterprises and for workers employed in such enterprises.

In promoting the economic development of a developing country, the need for increasing productive capacity is usually emphasized. However, expansion of the nation's capacity to supply goods and services cannot by itself bring about even development of the economy; there must also be balanced growth on the demand side. Not infrequently, developing countries find that traditional customs and social habits, religious beliefs, and sometimes a strong spirit of nationalism hinder the modernization of the mode of living among masses, which in turn prevents the introduction of modern consumption goods on a mass basis. In such a traditional society, a crucial role is played by mass education in reshaping the pattern of social behavior among the people and promoting the process of modernization; indeed, without modern education it is almost impossible to modernize the mode of living.

Over 70 per cent of households in Thailand are engaged in agriculture, and most farmers still continue to live in the same village of the past few generations, with little contact with the outside world. The proportion of the expenditures of these households on religious activity is relatively large in spite of their limited spendable resources, reflecting the deep faith of Thai farmers in Hinayana Buddhism.

There have been a number of studies of the traditional aspects of the way of life prevailing among the Thai people. Wendell Blanchard, in *Thailand, Its People, Its Society, Its Culture*, makes this observation:

> The social goal of the rural population, and also to a large extent of the urban population, remains the acquisition of merit and preparation for one's future existence. The financial investment is enormous; one source, for example, states that the cash outlays for merit-making range from 7 per cent to 84 per cent of the total cash expenditures of a single family, with the average around 25 per cent. The expenditure results in a general economic leveling of the Thai rural population; more than anything else it helps to maintain the classlessness characteristic of the rural society.[7]

A Ministry of Agriculture survey of 1953 reported that the Thai farmers spent 8 per cent of their cash income on religious obligations. While such religious expenditures, as pointed out above by Blanchard, have tended to narrow differences in the economic levels of Thai farmers, these same expenditures likewise have tended to reduce the total economic activity of individuals and of all the farmers year after year. When good weather and a plentiful supply of water produce a good harvest, Thai farmers, instead of saving an incremental income for the future, traditionally have increased their offerings to the monks, their donations to the Buddhist temple, and their outlays on other "merit-makings" for happiness in the next life. Or, they have wasted their incremental income on gamblings. Women have spent it on gold necklaces, earrings, and other accessories at Chin-Hang (the jewelers). By the time the next rainy season comes around, all the savings are gone. Thus, the benefits of their incremental income have been spent for nonproductive purposes, leaving their level of living unimproved.

There has been a very low propensity to save also among urban workers, partly because of the tardiness of Thailand in developing savings institutions.

---

7. Wendell Blanchard, *Thailand, Its People, Its Society, Its Culture*, (New Haven, Connecticut: Human Relations Area Files, Inc., 1958), p. 116.

Since the war, however, there have been considerable changes in the Thai patterns of living, particularly in and around Bangkok. Women's clothing styles have become westernized even in the provinces, and bicycles and motorcycles are now seen widely, as are fountain pens, watches, and cameras. In the countryside, galvanized-iron sheets are replacing roofs of palm leaves.

The 1962 Household Expenditure Survey conducted by the National Statistical Office points up some of the changes that have occurred in Thai consumption patterns. (*See Table 12.*)

Families living in villages of the northeast region had total expenditures averaging 407 baht (about $20 per month), including the rice withdrawn from storage for family use valued at 98 baht. Of this expenditure 26.4 baht, or 6.5 per cent, went for wedding, ceremony and funeral expenses and cash contributions to organizations and persons. Another 7 baht went for food and offerings to priests, bringing the total of ceremonial, charitable and religious expenditures to 8 per cent.

Families living in towns of the northeast region had monthly expenditures averaging 1,105 baht. However, in spite of their higher incomes, (roughly four times that of the rural families), the urban families in the northeast region spent only 4 per cent on ceremonial, charitable and religious items.

These contrasts indicate that traditional patterns of consumption have been undergoing perceptible changes outside the rural areas. Further evidence of this can be seen in other reporting in the Household Expenditures Survey of 1962. (*See Table 13.*) The proportion of families owning radios was 55.8 per cent in the Bangkok-Thonburi municipal area, 32.6 per cent in towns of the northeast region, and as low as 4.9 per cent in villages of the same region. The ownership of sewing machines shows much the same pattern, as does most of the other durables. (Bicycles, motorcycles and scooters are an interesting exception; ownership in these instances is slightly higher in the towns than in the Bangkok area.) Public education has been a factor of major importance underlying these changes in the Thai way of life and consumption patterns. It has helped generate among the people a desire to improve their living by spending more of their income on better food, clothing, and shelter, or by saving for the

Table 12: Average Monthly Family Expenditures, 1962
(baht)

	Bangkok-Thonburi Area		Northeast Region Towns		Northeast Region Villages	
Food & beverages	646.42	44.9%	436.71	39.4%	178.05	43.8%
Clothing & materials	128.49	8.9	155.58	14.1	67.47	16.6
Housing & furnishings	109.50	7.6	86.75	7.9	31.80	7.8
Household operations	123.93	8.6	62.18	5.6	9.45	2.3
Medical & personal care	95.07	6.7	72.11	6.5	23.59	5.8
Transportation	91.78	6.4	74.77	6.8	13.00	3.3
Reading, recreation, education	79.07	5.5	90.13	8.2	14.57	3.6
Tobacco & alcoholic drinks	66.05	4.6	56.25	5.1	16.58	4.1
Misc. household exp.	45.96	3.2	23.34	2.1	31.25	7.7
Gifts & contributions	35.71	2.5	34.11	3.1	19.40	4.8
Taxes	16.17	1.1	13.04	1.2	1.00	0.2
Total	1,438.15	100.0	1,104.97	100.0	406.46	100.0

SELECTED ITEMS

Hair waving & sets	7.99	0.6	4.37	0.4	1.00	0.2
Vehicles expenses	40.66	2.8	44.25	4.0	5.12	1.3
Cinema admissions	12.73	0.9	8.18	0.7	0.51	0.1
Other recreation expenses	7.19	0.5	13.31	1.2	2.91	0.7
Purchase of lottery tickets	25.62	1.8	10.25	0.9	3.12	0.8
Newspapers	7.51	0.5	4.10	0.4	0.09	–
Books & other reading material	1.74	0.1	2.29	0.2	0.08	–
School fees & other educational expenses	24.28	1.7	52.00	4.7	6.88	1.7
Weddings & ceremonies	23.99	1.7	10.15	0.9	13.93	3.4
Funeral expenses	3.63	0.3	0.16	–	0.03	–
Cash contribution to organizations	28.42	2.0	24.32	2.2	12.43	3.1
Food and offerings to priests	7.29	0.5	9.79	0.9	6.97	1.7

Sources: National Statistical Office, *Household Expenditure Survey; Bangkok-Thonburi Municipal Area*, pp. 21, 35-36; *Household Expenditures Survey; Northeast Region*, pp. 18-19, 38-39, and 43-44.

Table 13:   Family Ownership of Selected Durable Goods, 1962
             (percentage)

Items	Bangkok-Thonburi Area	Northeast Region Towns	Northeast Region Villages
Radio	55.8%	32.6%	4.9%
Television	14.4	0.6	–
Phonograph	4.7	2.2	0.2
Refrigerator	8.6	0.6	0.1
Washing machine	1.4	0.6	0.1
Electric fan	33.3	12.3	–
Air conditioner	0.6	0.3	–
Sewing machine	33.5	22.0	4.7
Automobile	7.4	3.9	0.3
Motorcycle and scooter	3.9	4.1	1.2
Bicycle	8.3	44.8	9.7
Camera	6.0	2.5	0.1

Sources: National Statistical Office, *Household Expenditure Survey; Bangkok-Thonburi Municipal Area*, p. 52; *Household Expenditure Survey; Northeast Region*, p. 62.

future, as against donations to the temple, offerings to priests or gambling. It is to be noted in this connection that the absence of rigid social stratification, as in the case of India's caste system, has made it possible for Thailand to assimilate modern ways more rapidly than other countries of Southeast Asia. Likewise, because Thailand was never a colony, it has not been subject to the excessive nationalism that has caused some newly independent countries to reject irrationally any influence from the former colonial powers. Furthermore, the Hinayana Buddhist faith has not acted as a strong deterrent to the advance of modernization in the Thai mode of living.

"Demonstration effects" have had much to do with the change in Thai consumption patterns during the postwar years. Over the last decade or two, the number of American and other foreign residents in Thailand has increased rapidly. As Bangkok is a center of international airways in Southeast Asia, millions of tourists have visited Bangkok or passed through. The number of foreign visitors attending international conferences has also increased since the United Nations Economic Commission for Asia and Far East (ECAFE) and many other international organizations have located their offices in Bangkok. Thus, the Thai people have had an increasing contact with foreign ways and styles. Thai students who have studied abroad also have helped to westernize the Thai living.

Motion pictures, radio and television have helped to westernize consumption patterns in the provinces. Because the development of electric utilities still lags in Thailand, transistor radios have been in great demand. In 1962, the government installed two television transmitters, one in the northeast and another in the southern region; the expansion of public power due to the completion of Bhumipol Dam has extended the geographic coverage of television in the country.

The changing patterns of consumption led first to an increase in the imports of such goods as fountain pens, bicycles, motorcycles, radios, etc. The need for the maintenance and repair of these consumer durables in turn brought about the establishment of small-scale repair shops, forerunner of Thailand's industrialization. This was followed by the construction of assembly plants for bicycles and then for automobiles. In a similar manner, once the Thai people who had depended on herb medicine had come to know the efficacy of vitamins and antibiotics imported from abroad after the war, the popular demand for these products led to the establishment of modern pharmaceutical manufacturing plants. And the increased use of galvanized iron sheets, in place of palm thatch roofing, led to the establishment of three plants for the manufacture of the galvanized sheets.

In other words, consumption expenditures have induced investment activity in Thailand, just as ordinarily observed in a modern industrial society where the acceleration principle operates. In an underdeveloped society, an increase in the consumption expenditure often tends not only to increase its demand for imports but also to contribute to its economic development in a negative way. Where disparity between the rich and the poor is great, the demand by a small wealthy class for more costly consumer goods tends to be reflected on the society's demand for imports, and does not necessarily generate productive investment at home. Demand for consumer goods can induce investment in productive facilities for such goods only if and when a sufficient market is developed. This condition is present in Thailand and is one of the main causes of the country's high economic growth rate, unequalled by other Southeast Asian countries.

It should be noted also that increased demand for consumption goods among the masses not only induces entrepreneurial investment but also stimulates the moral of the working masses. Instead of "merit-making" for happiness after death, they work to satisfy their worldly wants. The heightened morale of the workers raises their labor efficiency and encourages mobility. Shifts take place among the labor force from farming to mining, or road, dam, and other construction jobs. As for farmers, these new currents in society have stimulated them to shift from traditional to new agricultural methods, as has happened in most societies. The same drive, operating among the urban workers, has induced them to seek higher incomes through higher levels of education.

In conclusion, it is no exaggeration to say that a healthy expansion in the consumption by the masses of the people, by expanding capital investment on the one hand and bringing about an increased and improved labor force on the other, has led to a rise in productivity, a greater capacity to supply goods and services, and a rapid growth in the national economy of Thailand.

The Educational Policy of the Thai Government

The educational development undertaken over many years by the government of Thailand has been successful in gradually reducing the illiteracy rate among the Thai people. The literacy rate for those under 24 years of age is now better than 80 per cent, which suggests that as a result of the government's stepped-up efforts to develop education after the war there has been a growth in the number of those who have learned how to read and write and acquired some technical skills.

Industrialization of the Thai economy has experienced an increased tempo since the latter half of the 1950's. Textile mills and other modern factories have been constructed, and a comparatively efficient workforce has been obtained and is running these factories. On road and other construction jobs many properly trained engineers and technicians are being employed. Behind all these economic achievements lies an intensive effort on the part of the Thai government to develop education that has been going on since the constitutional revolution of 1932, and particularly since the educational reform of 1951.

In underdeveloped countries, scarcity of employment opportunities suitable for the young people with high education and technical skills not infrequently pushes them into a social group agitating for radical political and economic changes. Thailand, however, has been fortunate in having been able to provide its educated people with an increased demand for their capabilities. Indeed, the recent economic growth of the country has been so phenomenal that the requirement for able manpower has risen to an unprecedented degree.

The educational policy of the Thai government has been designed to meet manpower requirements generated by the high rate of economic growth in Thailand. The late Field Marshal Sarit, who did much to promote education for the people of Thailand while Prime Minister between 1959 and 1963, extended compulsory education from four to seven years. Field Marshall T. Kittikachorn has continued his predecessor's policy in placing great emphasis on educational development. In the first Central Government Budget presented by Field Marshal Kittikachorn's cabinet for fiscal 1965, education was allocated 17.5 per cent of the total budget, second only to the economic development which received 27.1 per cent.

The Second Five-Year National Economic and Social Development Plan (1966-1971) recognizes the importance of education as an integral part of socio-economic development of Thailand. The main objective is to provide an educational system which will develop the human resources to meet manpower requirements, facilitate transition in an era of technology, expand compulsory education, and improve facilities in order to accommodate the increasing number of students at all levels. In addition, improvement of quality is being given special emphasis in the development of education.

The physical targets in the development of education have been proposed as follows:

	1966			1971		
Education Level	Student Enrollment	No. of Teachers	No. of Schools	Student Enrollment	No. of Teachers	No. of Schools
Primary	4,768,000	108,083	24,718	5,504,000	213,851	29,087
General secondary	345,502	9,003	1,308	575,700	21,560	1,716
Vocational secondary	42,600	4,212	187	63,000	8,200	200
Teacher training	19,776	1,716	29	31,700	2,833	32
Advanced technical	8,460	475	6	19,090	2,009	10
University	33,531	1,266	5	43,830	3,500	9

Major educational development programs included in the Second Plan are:

Primary Education

The improvement and expansion of primary education is aimed at raising the national standard of universal education for the fourth-grade to the seventh-grade level, thus broadening the base of enrollment in the next higher level of education.

Secondary Education

At the secondary level, major efforts are to be made to expand comprehensive schools, so the students will be guided toward studies of practical utility; particular emphasis will be given to expansion of the vocational high schools. At the same time, the academic standard of general secondary education will be strengthened to meet pre-university requirements.

Teacher Training

Improvement and expansion of the teacher's training program are to be given high priority. At the technical-college level, a new college will be established at Tak, making a total of seven institutes of this kind.

Higher Education

The university-level education program will focus on the upgrading of quality of present institutions and on the decentralizing of higher education in regions outside Bangkok. Greater emphasis will be placed on technical curricula in engineering, agriculture, medicine, science, and other subjects for development purposes.

In order to achieve the above objectives and targets, the outlay for education has been set at about 6,520 million baht, which is almost triple the amount allocated during the First Plan. (See Table 14.)

Table 14: Sectoral Allocations of Development Expenditures Under the First and Second Development Plans

(millions of baht)

Sector	First Plan 1961-1966		Second Plan 1967-1971	
Agriculture	4,600	14.15%	11,300	20.23%
Industry and Mining	2,600	7.94	885	1.58
Power	4,300	13.26	3,540	6.31
Transportation and communications	10,200	31.42	17,080	30.58
Commerce	—	—	180	0.32
Community facilities	5,500	16.74	10,250	18.35
Health	1,400	4.18	2,570	4.60
Education	2,500	7.63	6,520	11.67
Unallocated	1,500	4.78	3,550	6.37
Total	32,600	100.00	55,875	100.00

Source: The National Economic Development Board, Office of the Prime Minister, *Summary of the Second Five-Year Plan (1967-1971)*, October 1966.

Requirements for professional, technical, and skilled manpower will be met by expanding university education and also the Thailand Productivity Center. During the period covered by the Plan, the Center will expand its activities to provide training for about 5,000 managerial personnel. At the same time, a large number of administrative personnel and officers of various government departments, as well as from private industry, will be selected for training abroad in their respective fields of specialization.

For middle-level manpower, the World Bank has approved a loan for improvement of the vocational education. The United States and other countries have given grants in the educational and training sector. It is clear that for the further development of education in Thailand, assistance from foreign countries and international organizations will continue to be necessary.

The Role of the Thai-Chinese

The economic development of a low-income country requires the presence of a socially conscious elite to provide national leadership. The elite in such a situation must possess the courage to tear down old habits and customs and introduce a modern economic system and the capabilities to build new organizations, operate productive enterprises; and make an effective use of superior technology available to the country.

The ethnic Thai, however, generally lack entrepreneurial spirit, and within the upper classes there is a strong tendency to look down on manual labor. This is compounded by a lack of the necessary knowledge and ability for carrying on commercial and industrial activities.

In Thailand the role of the elite in economic development has been discharged by the Chinese community, which dates back hundreds of years. There are a number of Chinese millionaires who achieved their status through hard and enduring work, starting off sometimes as laborers on irrigation projects in central Thailand, sometimes as peddlers. Some of them now own textile mills, chemical firms, and banks, while others operate rubber plantations and orchards. Still others work as operatives in rubber selection plants. Thus, the Chinese and their descendants have exhibited an excellent capability and vitality as workers, technicians, professionals, or owner managers. It is to be noted that the emphasis placed by the Chinese on the education of their children has contributed a great deal to their attainment of status and wealth.

Chinese settled in Thailand many centuries ago. When the southward-moving Thai people living in southern China reached the Chao Phraya Delta in the thirteenth century, they found Chinese already trading in the Gulf ports. Around 1660, the Chinese population in Thailand is said to have numbered about 10,000, many of them were engaged in mercantile activities with ties to the Thai royal monopoly over trading and other areas of the economy.

The Bowring Treaty of 1855 abolished the royal trading monopolies, and thereafter the government farmed out to the Chinese a large number of concessions for the collection of various taxes and trade duties. The Bowring Treaty also lifted the royal export restrictions on rice, and the production of rice in Thailand increased in response to an increase in demand overseas. The gainers were again the Chinese tradesmen, who were in charge of the collection, transport, refining, and export of rice.

Few Chinese women emigrated to Thailand before 1893, and even afterward they comprised only about 10 per cent of the total number of Chinese immigrants to Thailand. As a result, Chinese male immigrants usually married ethnic Thai women, and their descendants began to feel a greater allegiance to Thailand than to China.

The assimilated Chinese population in Thailand, which has retained many of the characteristics of the ethnic Chinese, have a position of leadership in Bangkok politics and business as well as in provincial business enterprise. They now play leading roles as a new elite in Thai society. Meanwhile, the ethnic Thai aristocracy, the traditional elite of the country, gravitate toward military, government, and religious occupations.

While the second and third generation Chinese population has been for the most part assimilated in Thai society, there is another group of Chinese residents that has not been so assimilated, just as is seen in other parts of Southeast Asia. The establishment of such unassimilated overseas Chinese community in Thailand has been mainly due to the continuous arrival of new immigrants from mainland China, bringing with them the traditions and customs of their country.

Stronger pressure from the Thai led to a greater cohesion among the people in the overseas Chinese community in an effort to defend themselves. These Chinese immigrants cherished a hope of returning home in wealth and glory, and indeed the total amount of cash remitted home by such Chinese communities in Southeast Asia was staggering, Thailand being no exception.

Thailand maintained a favorable trade balance before World War II. Much of the nation's export earnings, however, ended in the hands of the Chinese immigrant community, which remitted a major portion of them back home, and thus contributed nothing to the capital accumulation in Thailand. This was one of the decisive factors responsible for retarding the economic progress of prewar Thailand.

A revision of the Immigration Act in November 1948, however, had a great impact on the overseas Chinese community in Thailand. Whereas there had been as many as 150,000 Chinese immigrants a year in the 1920's, the enactment of the new immigration law reduced the number of Chinese immigrants to 200 per year, just as in the case of the other foreign immigrants. As a result of this legislative action on the part of the Thai government, the traditional overseas Chinese community seems destined to be merged into the assimilated Chinese society in Thailand.

After the establishment of the People's Government at Peking in October 1949, there was a big reduction in the total amount of cash remitted home by the overseas Chinese in Thailand, and an increase was seen in their capital invested in Thailand. However, since competition had been becoming keener in mercantile activity, they sought new fields of investment. This helped bring about the establishment of a variety of manufacturing and machine-repair shops, though small in the scale of operation. For instance, some Chinese bicycle importers started bicycle-repair shops, while Chinese wholesalers and retailers of plastic pipes went into manufacturing themselves by importing plastic injection and moulding machinery. Thus, there has been a gradual shift in the weight of the overseas Chinese capital from the commercial to the industrial sector in Thailand.

The establishment by the government in 1959 of the Board of Investment, together with the adoption of various measures for the promotion of industry, stimulated private capital investment in Thailand by Japan and other foreign countries. It is important to remember that much of this foreign investment has been made with the assistance of the Chinese entrepreneurs, often through the setting up of joint ventures with them. The Chinese capital, which had retarded the economic development of prewar Thailand, has now become an important generator of further economic growth in postwar Thailand. It is also important to note that there has been a significant amount of Chinese capital flowing into Thailand from Hongkong and Taiwan. Thus, the over-all contributions made by the Chinese in Thailand to the rapid industrialization and economic growth of the country has been very substantial since the war.

In some countries of Southeast Asia, a strong sense of nationalism continuing after independence forced the Chinese out of business so as to replace them with ethnic nationals. However, these measures caused economic confusion and contributed to a slow-down of the economic progress in these countries, since the new owners and managers lacked the entrepreneurial ability of the Chinese. In Thailand, however, there were hardly any measures adopted by the governments to eliminate the influence of the Chinese already living in the country, and the Chinese have become assimilated in Thai society to a considerable extent. Appreciable credit should be given to the Thai policy, direct and indirect, of encouraging for the economic development of the country the assimilation of the Chinese population, with their high calibre, vitality, and capital, into the Thai society.

Foreign Private Investment and Economic Development

There is no doubt that an inflow of private capital from Europe in prewar days contributed in some measure to the economic development of Thailand. However, the magnitude of the foreign private investment in prewar Thailand was insignificant as compared with that in other colonial territories of Southeast Asia, as Thailand has long been an independent nation. Especially, since the worldwide crisis of the 1930's, there had been a big reduction in the outflow of capital from western European countries to Southeast Asia, and Thailand was no exception to this.

It is only recently, since rapid economic progress has continued to be observed in Thailand, that private capital investment has been stepped up from abroad. This occurred around 1960 when the industrial development of the country began to show a phenomenal rise. In 1958, for instance, the combined total of the direct investment and other private long- and short-term loans from abroad was 363.1 million baht, but the figure increased to 448.7 million baht in 1960, rose to 756.6 million baht the following year, and jumped all the way to 1,505.6 million baht in 1962. Foreign private investment in Thailand has been maintained since then at a high level.

Before the 1950's, foreign capital investment was often made in commerce and other nonindustrial sectors of the Thai economy. Since 1960, however, the private capital from abroad, often accompanied by new industrial technology, has been instrumental in opening modern factories in Thailand.

State Enterprises and Industrial Development of Thailand

In a developing country there is no other alternative but for the state initially to develop its modern industry, as the country is without the economic or legal preparation for the introduction of private industrial capital from abroad. Thailand was no exception, and modern industrial development was for the most part undertaken initially by the state. State enterprises were established to manufacture gunny bags, cotton textiles, sugar, paper, ceramics, tobacco, cement, steel, alum, plywood, etc. Except for the tobacco enterprise, which was guaranteed a monopoly by the Monopoly Act, and except for a few other industries such as cement, where productive efficiency was maintained at a high level following the government's participation, most of these state enterprises were inefficient in operation. Because they imposed a financial burden on the government, some of them were sold to private investors, while others were simply shut down.

It is to be noted that the reasons for the failure of these state enterprises lay in the inefficient management and the lack of technical maturity that are often associated with the state enterprise everywhere. In the hiring of both production and nonproduction workers, state enterprises often gave a priority to personal relations and considerations other than those of worker qualification and ability, thus lowering labor efficiency. The basic criterion of profitability in purchasing raw materials and parts also was often ignored, which increased cost of production to a marked degree.

Thus, it may be said that the government's efforts to develop modern industry through state enterprises generally resulted in failure. Nevertheless, due credit should be given to the educative role played by these state enterprises as a forerunner of the modern industry in Thailand. Had it not been for such experience, the government would have found it very difficult to formulate and set up an effective industrial development policy oriented toward a full participation and utilization of private capital, both domestic and foreign.

Industrial Development Under the Sarit and Kittikachorn Governments

While the state enterprises were going through a difficult time as a pioneer of the modern industrial development in Thailand, Chinese merchants and manufacturers living there were expanding their investment in small-scale industry. It was after the successful coup d'etat in October 1958 by the late Field Marshal Sarit that private investment in large-scale industry began to develop in Thailand. Starting with Revolutionary Proclamation No. 33, the government took positive measures for the promotion of private industrial investment. The Board of Investment was set up, and it efficiently processed those applications by private investors for the granting of promotional privileges.[8]

It is true that there had been an earlier Industrial Promotion Act, issued by the government in October 1954, but its frequent interference with private enterprises had the effect of deterring rather than encouraging the inflow of foreign capital into the country. As a consequence, the number of applications granted promotional privileges by the Ministry of Industry under this act was only eleven, and of these only two had been granted before the late Field Marshal Sarit came to power in February 1959. However, between April 1959, when the Board of Investment was established, and October 1960, no less than 74 applications were granted promotional privileges under Proclamation No. 33. On October 25, 1960, the Promotion of Industrial Investment Act was proclaimed by the Thai Revolutionary Government, and there were revisions in this act on

---

8. Revolutionary Proclamation No. 33 of December 5, 1958, set out the fundamental policy for industrial development and capital import to be carried out by the government of Thailand, and also simplified the existing legal procedures affecting private investment in Thailand. In particular, the government has been required by the Proclamation to grant equal rights to both Thai and foreign investors in Thai industry. Moreover, the Proclamation made clear that the government would not nationalize those private enterprises or establish any state enterprises that would compete with them. The private enterprises thus encouraged were guaranteed many privileges, including exemption from and reduction of import duties on machinery, component parts, and accessories; the right to remit profits abroad and repatriation of capital; and the right to bring in from abroad experts and skilled workers beyond the immigration quota. The Proclamation also guaranteed that the state would assist these enterprises by placing import restrictions and increasing import duties on those goods that would compete with them.
Revolutionary Proclamation No. 47, issued on January 12, 1959, permitted the foreign firms granted promotional privileges to acquire necessary amounts of land beyond the limit placed on the foreigners in the existing land ordinance.

February 9, 1962, to simplify legal procedures associated with applications under the act and grant more promotional privileges to the private investors. The number of parties granted promotional privileges under this act from October 1960 to the end of 1963 totaled 157, though it must be understood that not all those granted promotional privileges necessarily have set up enterprises and brought them into successful operation. (See Appendix.) In all, the Board of Investment has issued 390 promotion certificates to various companies, with total working capital amounting to 10,000 million baht, since the adoption of the Industrial Promotion Act in 1960.

Private capital investment prior to 1959 was limited for the most part to relatively few fields of industrial activity, such as rice processing, lumbering, distilling, sugar refining, textile weaving, and so on. However, those new enterprises set up under the government policy since 1959 have gone into more diverse fields of industrial activity, including automobile assembly and metal refining. Instead of small-scale plants operated by overseas Chinese, large-scale factories with modern machinery and equipment and new technology have been established. The government policy since 1959 has thus made a great contribution to the rapid growth and diversification as well as modernization of Thai industry.

These efforts in industrial development have made Thailand self-sufficient in such goods as cotton yarn (No. 46 count or less), galvanized sheet iron, nails cement, sugar, medium-quality paper, gunny bags, sulphuric acid, condiments, and glass bottles. And the rate of self-sufficiency has been rising rapidly for a number of other items, including tin-plate sheets, electric wire, blankets, plywood, electric bulbs, batteries, pharmaceutical products. As a consequence, in its 1962 revision of the Promotion of Industrial Investment Act, the government withdrew 24 industries from the list of those to be aided under the act; these included sulphuric acid, sugar, condiments, plywood, cement, and nails. The decision was based on the understanding by the government that the enterprises already granted promotional privileges either had the capacity, or planned to increase their capacity sufficiently, to meet present

Table 15: Growth in Output of Chief Manufactured Goods, 1956-66

Year	Cement (metric tons)	Cotton Textiles (1,000 sq. yards)	Gunny Bags (1,000 units)	Sugar (1,000 metric tons)	Paper (metric tons)	Tobacco (metric tons)
1956	397,608	n.a.	3,561	54	2,732	8,461
1957	402,211	n.a.	3,566	65	2,800	8,820
1958	498,865	n.a.	4,517	80	2,809	8,479
1959	566,395	n.a.	5,060	120	2,585	8,441
1960	544,977	n.a.	6,877	140	2,554	8,886
1961	800,284	86,588	8,842	150	3,627	9,739
1962	967,475	109,437	10,815	151	5,768	10,525
1963	997,231	140,046	23,128	125	7,890	10,148
1964	1,059,136	189,399	33,511	167	13,577	10,409
1965	1,247,997	237,069	40,360	319	13,330	10,057
1966	1,475,712	–	42,597	269	12,241	11,123

Source: Bank of Thailand, *Monthly Report* (March 1967), p. 64.

domestic demand for those products, and that, therefore, government assistance would no longer be necessary in those industries. An increasing number of industries have since been withdrawn from the promotable list, and there is even a problem of surplus production in sugar-refining and a few other industries. Thus, the government's policy for industrial promotion in Thailand must be selective rather than general, as it has been.

Foreign Capital and Industrial Development of Thailand

We have observed how effective the government's policy for industrial promotion has been in recent years in stimulating the inflow of foreign private capital and advancing the industrial development of Thailand. We can now examine the nationality and nature of such foreign private capital in relation to Thailand's economic structure and development.

The number of applications by foreign firms, made either independently or through joint ventures, that were granted promotional privileges by the Board of Investment between 1959 and 1963 totaled about 150. This means that there were only a few Thai applications approved for promotional privileges. Of all the successful applications, 59 were made by Chinese investors including Chinese residing in Thailand, while 25 were made by Japanese investors. These were followed by 16 applications from the United States, 10 from Great Britain, 6 from Denmark, 5 from India, and 4 from Portugal, Switzerland, and West Germany.

Although it is hard to give accurate totals of proposed investment country by country, rough calculations show that the Chinese surpassed all the others with 350 million baht, followed by Japan with 180 million baht. Some 80 million baht were recorded for the United States, 45 million for Denmark, and 30 million for Switzerland.

Thailand's heavy reliance on foreign capital in developing its modern industry generated a new problem in the country. Although foreign private investment, as pointed out earlier, involved a wide variety of industries, these have been predominantly in the nature of import substitution. New firms thus established are large-scale operations and have a nationwide market.

They coexist with many petty cottage industries and local shops, thus creating a dual structure in Thailand's economy. There have been also some instances in which large-scale enterprises forced small firms out of market, a situation that will perhaps continue for some time.

The establishment of large-scale production in Thailand is not without problems. Deficiency of social overhead investment in the country presents a number of difficulties for the operation of larger manufacturing establishments. It is expected, of course, that such difficulties will gradually disappear with an increase in the government resources available for social investments as the Thai economy grows. Further foreign economic aid and cooperation programs will also contribute to the expansion of highway construction and other social investments in the country. Similar expectations can be entertained with respect to raising the level of technical education among the Thai people.

Another important problem arises from the use by Thailand of protectionism and other measures to encourage import-substitution and thus reduce the imports that the country had heavily relied on to meet its domestic demand. It is true that such measures have saved Thailand considerable foreign exchange, but if the industries that have been brought into being by these means are to become foreign exchange earners they will have to be made highly competitive internationally. The current industrial strength of Thailand is such, however, that it would be extremely difficult for the country to export its industrial goods in competition with the industrially advanced countries. This is indeed a hard task facing Thailand, its people and government.

The recent economic development of Thailand shows that the country has succeeded in developing its modern industry, with the assistance of foreign capital and technical know-how, through the modernization of the consumption patterns of the masses of the people, which in turn has induced investments in the consumer goods industry. Such investment was at first concentrated in the final stages of the production process, but gradually moved toward earlier stages of production, yielding higher added value per unit of capital invested and leading to the supply of raw materials and parts at home rather than from abroad. Now attention should be paid to the construction of chemical and metal refining plants to meet the growing demand for such materials on the part of new factories recently set up in Thailand.

With the aid of foreign loans and technical cooperation, the government of Thailand has just completed Bhumipol Dam, and the further industrialization of Thailand will make a more effective use of the increased supply of electrical power generated in the country. The industrialization also will continue, as it has in the past, to expand opportunities of modern employment for the Thai people and stimulate among them a desire to receive a more and improved technical and vocational education.

Thus, Thailand's strategy for economic development has so far exhibited a great many achievements. Probably no other strategy could have furthered more successfully the economic development of Thailand. It seems apparent that in any country the restriction of consumption together with forced savings for the sake of a rapid rate of capital formation at home will lead to a narrow domestic market for the goods produced at home; this will soon bring to a standstill the economic expansion of the country. However, since import substitution has been the main drive behind Thailand's industrialization, its industry will encounter many difficulties before becoming competitive on the international market. Solution to this enormous problem will probably entail a genuine international cooperation, particularly by the industrially advanced countries of the world.

In this respect, some hints may be derived from the modern history of Japanese industries, which started out far behind the Western powers, but have risen to their present level of progress thanks to years of diligent toil by the workers. For a century, Japan has struggled hard to develop the export market for its products in stiff competition with advanced Western powers and has succeeded in becoming a major exporter of industrial products. It behooves Thailand, therefore, to introduce foreign technology in a vigorous manner, enhance labor efficiency, produce superior industrial products at low costs, and develop the capacity to export them at low prices.

As for export markets, Thailand would do well to look to Japan, as well as to the underdeveloped countries in Asia and Africa. Japan, with nearly 100 million people who are increasing their income year after year at a considerable rate, should provide a good market not only for Thailand's primary products but also for its industrial goods—especially labor-intensive prod-

Table 16: Japanese Share of Thailand's Total Trade
(millions of baht)

Year	Thailand's Exports			Thailand's Imports		
	Total	To Japan	% of Total	Total	From Japan	% of Total
1957	7,540	595	7.9%	8,537	1,746	20.5%
1958	6,447	486	7.5	8,237	1,890	22.9
1959	7,560	888	11.7	8,988	2,256	25.1
1960	8,629	1,530	17.7	9,622	2,463	25.6
1961	9,997	1,481	14.8	10,287	2,953	28.7
1962	9,529	1,352	14.2	11,504	3,357	29.2
1963	9,676	1,826	18.9	12,803	4,073	31.8
1964	12,339	2,673	21.7	14,253	4,704	33.0
1965	12,941	2,359	18.2	16,185	5,200	32.1

Source: Thailand Customs Department.

Table 17: Share of Thailand's Total Exports of Primary Products,[a] Going to Japan, 1957-65
(metric tons)

Year	Rubber Total Exports	Rubber To Japan	Rubber % of Total	Maize Total Exports	Maize To Japan	Maize % of Total	Tapioca Products Total Exports	Tapioca Products To Japan	Tapioca Products % of Total	Jute & Kenaf Total Exports	Jute & Kenaf To Japan	Jute & Kenaf % of Total
1957	134,833	57	0.04%	64,337	36,393	56.6%	98,775	899	0.9%	14,580	3,706	25.4%
1958	135,508	368	0.3	162,914	129,683	79.6	151,626	981	0.6	27,587	3,352	12.2
1959	174,404	16,578	9.5	236,781	189,185	79.9	194,648	1,631	0.8	37,317	5,282	14.2
1960	169,655	40,717	24.0	514,745	441,046	85.7	270,758	1,279	0.5	61,769	13,523	21.9
1961	184,598	44,926	24.3	567,236	405,403	71.5	443,362	8,546	1.9	143,477	28,777	20.1
1962	194,180	50,742	26.1	472,405	229,676	48.6	400,788	7,688	1.9	237,898	35,613	15.0
1963	186,887	62,478	33.4	744,046	453,414	60.9	427,443	14,590	3.4	125,753	30,366	24.1
1964	216,994	80,813	37.2	1,115,041	844,936	75.8	738,859	65,509	8.9	162,095	38,642	23.8
1965	210,854	54,178	25.7	804,380	559,746	69.6	719,442	19,084	2.7	316,986	60,988	19.2

[a] Not including rice and tea

Source: Bank of Thailand, *Monthly Report* (March 1967).

ucts. Thailand's emerging industries should try to develop the rapidly expanding Japanese market in competition with those of Hongkong, Taiwan, and the Republic of Korea. (*See Tables 16 and 17.*)

APPENDIX

YEARLY CAPITAL EXPENDITURES ON NEW FACILITES IN THAILAND UNDER THE INDUSTRIAL PROMOTION ACT OF 1958 AND THE PROMOTION OF INDUSTRIAL INVESTMENT ACT OF 1960

Appendix Table: Number of Firms Opening (A) or Adding (B) New Facilities and Their Estimated Capital Expenditures (C)

(thousands of baht)

Industry	1959 A No.	1959 A C	1959 B No.	1959 B C	1960 A No.	1960 A C	1960 B No.	1960 B C	1961 A No.	1961 A C	1961 B No.	1961 B C	1962 A No.	1962 A C	1962 B No.	1962 B C
Textiles	4	30,000	2	9,000	3	25,000	4	5,500	3	25,400	3	3,700			3	13,700
Automobile assembly	1	5,070			3	27,000							3	35,530		
Auto parts & accessories									1	2,000	1	2,500	1	1,000	1	1,000
Woodworking			1	1,000	1	2,000							1	5,000		
Farm products storage									2	12,000			1	12,000		
Electrical products					1	3,400			2	6,800			1	4,500		
Paint & ink									2	10,000						
Fasteners																
Canning																
Ceramics															1	3,000
Rubber shoes & tires	1	3,000	1	5,000			1	3,000								
Paper products													2	12,000		
Radio assembly													1	2,500		
Cement							1	72,000			1	20,000			1	16,000
Bamboo wares													2	1,500		
Plastics													1	11,000		
Glass					1	6,000			1	3,000						

212

Pharmaceutical products	2	166,488									
Vegetable oil		23,000	1	10,500	1						
Milk	1								1	750	
Edible flour	1	25,000	1	3,000	3	28,821	1	5,000	2	43,000	
Cold storage									1	3,440	
Electrical wires			2	5,000					2	2,800	
Sugar	2	42,000	5	89,000	3	20,500	3	30,800	2	25,000	
Battery	1	10,000	1	400							
Coconut fibre	1	418	1	6,000							1 5,000
Gunny bags			1	40,000							
Fishing net			1	8,000					1	20,000	
Iron products	2	11,000	2	37,500			2	4,000	1	10,000	
Oil tanks	1	5,000							2	11,200	
Chemical products	1	12,000			1	2,000	2	7,000	1	1,000	
Gypsum			1	30,000							
Plywood											
Meat packing							1	50,000			
Pearl culture							1	2,000			
Tea							1	2,000			
Oil refinery							1	10,000	1	15,000	
Sewing machine assembly									1	5,000	
Metal smelting & refining											
Chemical fertilizers											
Miscellaneous products							1	1,000	5	15,500	1 1,200
Total est. capital expenditures		166,488		29,400		281,800		131,821		164,000	33,200		237,720	1	39,900
		195,888				413,621				197,200		277,620	

Appendix Table (Continued)

Industry	1963 No.	1963 A C	1963 B No.	1963 B C	Total A	Total B (1959-1963)
Textiles	6	83,000	6	2,227		
Automobile assembly	1	5,000				
Auto parts & accessories	2	7,000				
Woodworking	3	6,500				
Farm products storage						
Electrical products	3	10,500	1	1,125		
Paint & ink	2	14,000				
Fasteners			1	2,500		
Canning	2	12,500				
Ceramics	1	10,000				
Rubber shoes & tires	2	22,000				
Paper products						
Radio assembly	1	3,000	1	30,000		
Cement						
Bamboo wares	2	1,400				
Plastics	1	10,000				
Glass	1	12,000				

214

Pharmaceutical products					
Vegetable oil	1	2,000			
Milk	3	26,000			
Edible flour					
Cold storage	1	3,000			
Electrical wires					
Sugar					
Battery	2	5,000			
Coconut fibre	2	36,000			
Gunny bags			1	5,000	
Fishing net			1	1,000	
Iron products	7	57,400			
Oil tanks					
Chemical products					
Gypsum					
Plywood					
Meatpacking					
Pearl culture	1	2,000			
Tea					
Oil refinery					
Sewing machine assembly					
Metal smelting & refining	2	18,500			
Chemical fertilizers	1	120,000			
Miscellaneous products	1	3,000			
Total est. capital expenditures		469,800		41,852	1,319,808	276,173
		511,652			1,595,981	

Source: Government of Japan, Ministry of Foreign Affairs, Bureau of Economic Affairs, Asia Section, *Foreign Enterprises in Thailand*, July 1964, Table 3, pp. 21-22.

OTHER SUPPLEMENTARY PAPERS PUBLISHED BY CED

To order CED publications please indicate number in column entitled "# Copies Desired." Then mail this order form and check for total amount in envelope to Distribution Division, CED, 477 Madison Ave., New York, 10022.

Order Number   **Copies Desired**

1S . . THE ECONOMICS OF A FREE SOCIETY
William Benton
October, 1944, 20 pages. (20¢)

6S . . THE CHANGING ECONOMIC FUNCTION
OF THE CENTRAL CITY
Raymond Vernon
January, 1959, 92 pages, 14 tables, 8 charts. ($1.25)

7S . . METROPOLIS AGAINST ITSELF
Robert C. Wood
March, 1959, 56 pages. ($1.00)

8S . . TRENDS IN PUBLIC EXPENDITURES
IN THE NEXT DECADE
Otto Eckstein
April, 1959, 56 pages, 28 tables, 2 charts. ($1.00)

10S . . DEVELOPING THE "LITTLE" ECONOMIES
Donald R. Gilmore
April, 1960, 160 pages, 20 tables. ($2.00)

11S . . THE EDUCATION OF BUSINESSMEN
Leonard S. Silk
December, 1960, 48 pages, 9 tables. (75¢)

13S . . THE SOURCES OF ECONOMIC GROWTH
IN THE UNITED STATES AND THE ALTERNATIVES BEFORE US
Edward F. Denison
January, 1962, 308 pages, 4 charts, 33 tables. ($4.00)

14S . . COMPARATIVE TARIFFS AND TRADE—
THE U.S. AND THE EUROPEAN COMMON MARKET
Prepared by Frances K. Topping
March, 1963, over 1,000 pages. ($37.50)

15S . . FARMING, FARMERS, AND MARKETS
FOR FARM GOODS
Karl A. Fox, Vernon W. Ruttan, Lawrence W. Witt
November, 1962, 190 pages, 16 charts, 46 tables. ($3.00)

16S . . THE COMMUNITY ECONOMIC BASE STUDY
Charles M. Tiebout
December, 1962, 98 pages, 6 charts, 12 tables. ($1.50)

SEE OTHER SIDE⟶

17S . . HOW A REGION GROWS—
AREA DEVELOPMENT IN THE U.S. ECONOMY
Harvey S. Perloff, with Vera W. Dodds
March, 1963, 152 pages, 21 charts, 23 tables. ($2.25)

18S . . COMMUNITY ECONOMIC DEVELOPMENT EFFORTS:
FIVE CASE STUDIES
W. Paul Brann, V. C. Crisafulli, Donald R. Gilmore,
Jacob J. Kaufman, Halsey R. Jones, Jr., J. W. Milliman,
John H. Nixon, W. G. Pinnell
December, 1964, 352 pages, 47 tables, 14 charts. ($2.75)

19S . . CRISIS IN WORLD COMMUNISM—
MARXISM IN SEARCH OF EFFICIENCY
Frank O'Brien
January, 1965, 192 pages. ($2.75)

20S . . MEN NEAR THE TOP:
FILLING KEY POSTS IN THE FEDERAL SERVICE
John J. Corson and R. Shale Paul
April, 1966, 192 pages. ($3.00)

21S . . ECONOMIC DEVELOPMENT ISSUES:
LATIN AMERICA
Roberto Alemann (Argentina); Mario Henrique Simonsen
(Brazil); Sergio Undurraga Saavedra (Chile); Hernan
Echavarria (Colombia); Gustavo Romero Kolbeck
(Mexico); Romulo A. Ferrero (Peru).
August, 1967, 356 pages, 74 tables. ($4.25)

22S . . REGIONAL INTEGRATION AND
THE TRADE OF LATIN AMERICA
Roy Blough and Jack N. Behrman; Rómulo A. Ferrero
January, 1968, 184 pages, 14 tables. ($2.50)

23S . . FISCAL ISSUES IN THE FUTURE OF FEDERALISM
Metropolitan Case Studies; The Potential Impact of General Aid in Four Selected States; The Outlook for State and Local Finance.
May, 1968, 288 pages, 56 tables. ($3.00)

24S . . REMAKING THE INTERNATIONAL MONETARY SYSTEM: THE RIO AGREEMENT AND BEYOND
Fritz Machlup
June, 1968, 176 pages, 2 tables. ($3.00)

25S . . ECONOMIC DEVELOPMENT ISSUES: GREECE,
ISRAEL, TAIWAN, THAILAND
Diomedes D. Psilos (Greece); Nadav Halevi (Israel); Shigeto Kawano (Taiwan); Katsumi Mitani (Thailand)
September, 1968, 232 pages, 49 tables. ($4.00)

☐ P   bill me. (Remittance requested for orders under $3.00)
☐ I   me CED's current publications list.
☐ I   'o know how I might receive all of CED's future publications
   by   a Participant in the CED Reader-Forum.

* Hard cover edition available. Prices on request.